# Living
# A Spiritual Life
# In A
# Material World

DISCARD

## Practical Guidance
## In Light Of Kriya Yoga

## Rudra Shivananda

## Alight Publications
## 2018

# Living A Spiritual Life In A Material World

## By Rudra Shivananda

First Edition Published in September 2018

Alight Publications
PO Box 277
Live Oak, CA 95953

http://www.alightbooks.com

Softback ISBN: 978-1-931833-53-0
Ebook ISBN: 978-1-931833-54-7

Printed in the United States of America

To all Brothers & Sisters
on the path to
Self-Realization

# Contents

## Living A Spiritual Life In A Material World

## Part 3: Inspiration

## Part 4: Ethics

## Part 5: Beliefs

## Part 6: Spiritual Practice

## Part 7: Life and Living

## Conclusion - Beginning /208

## More Books by the Author /210

## About the Author /211

# Introduction

The great sages of all traditions have taught that our true nature is Spirit. An eternal, blissful and changeless Being – out True Self – pure consciousness. The enigma we are all faced with is that we do not experience this undifferentiated state of pure awareness but are suffering in the differentiated state of limited mind and sensory objects. How this came about is a mystery beyond the understanding of our three dimensional and time based mind. When we realize our nature as Spirit, we are able to know but still cannot describe this understanding in words or thoughts – 'those who know speak it not and those who speak about it know it not'.

The advise of the sages is to discover the truth for ourselves through a path or practice that can help us overcome our delusions, illusions and confusions, to realize our true nature. In the sanatana dharma of India, this is often the path of yoga, a system that has been proven and continuously modified to suit new generations of seekers while retaining its core essence. However, the spiritual practices themselves are only part of the path – the very life of the seeker is the other part, since we are children of Earth.

The material world is the body-mind-soul complex whereas our True Nature is non-material Spirit. We experience the material world with our sensory mind and the enveloping egocentric perspective. The soul is the apparent self identifying wth the body-mind and dominated by the abrogating ego. Our daily activites tend to rely on the sensory mind, strengthening the ego through taking possessions and credit for actions – this is my car and I did a great job to get the contract. We bask in the praise and get angry with criticisms. Desires are created when something is lacking or deemed inferior – we want a new and faster car. Our unenlightened actions create entanglements of cause and effect called karma that leads to a cycle of suffering – of death and rebirth.

A spiritual path and the practices along the path generally diminishes the pull of the sensory mind and the dominance of the ego. Spiritual practices develop the wisdom mind and leads the soul to one's True Nature or Spirit. However, there are pitfalls along the path.

Even meditation and yogic techniques can lead to strengthening of the ego. Recent studies among Buddhist meditators trained in the Western mode have shown inflated self-esteem in opposition to the lauded humility of the past. Traditionally, the Master or teacher had been the instrument to remind the student of the dangers of the ego and the need for sefl-lessness.

On the other hand, extreme non-attachment in yogic students can lead to apathy and depression. We need to be constantly reminded that we still have a body and need to live and function in the material world. Traditionally, the path of service or karma yoga was a means to offset this otherworldly tendency.

Another problem with spiritual practice is the attachment to tools such as the yoga postures, breathing techniques or visualizations other than focusing on the goal or outcome. Of course, attachment to the goal of spiritual practice can aslo become a hurdle to Self-Realization and a happy life!

In order to balance the spiritual life within the matrix of materiality, it is useful to develop within a model that encompassess both facets. I call this the Intentional Life Model ( refer Figure 1) which shows how to integrate our life actions into a wholeness to bring about a consciouness of our True Nature as well as the practical wisdom to live in the world as a spiritual Being.

The Intentional Life Model has the following seven interelated modes of being:

1.      Consciousness and Awareness: As we evolve, we become more and more aware of reality and overome the illusions of egocenters that divides us and make us miserable. We realize our unity with the universal field of consciousness and grow our limited

mind.

2.      Values: our spiritual progress is also marked by our cultivation of conscious values that correspond with our higher states of consciousness and the removal of unconscious biases. We need to understand our biases and values.

3.      Inspiration: The seeker often descends into apathy or depression due to the pressures of the sensory world. Therefore, it is necessary to have help along the way. This help can come in many forms and we should actually seek out the books, videos and workshops of spiritual people, whether fellow students, teachers or Masters. Constantly surround yourself with inspiration.

4.      Ethics: The spiritual path is full of pitfalls and traps because of our ego-mind and material desires. It is necessary to live life by a code of ethics that has been verified and handed down by the sages.

5.      Beliefs: Our minds are programmed with many confusing and opposing concepts that in the course of living in a particular cultural silo can lead to the accumulation of detrimental beliefs that can be hurdles on the spiritual path.

6.      Spiritual Path: The evolutionary impetus to achieve higher conccsiousness needs to be nurtured and grown through a sustained regular effort. It is not enough to have a spiritual path, one must continuously invoke the divine guide within us with a proven set of techniques handed down by the sages. There arc a variety of such spiritual practices depending on the temperament of the seeker..The specific one that I've settled on is called Kundalini Kriya Yoga, but I've sampled various yogic, Buddhist and Taoist modalities before settling on the one that resonates best with me.

7.      Life and Living: The level of our consciousness, our values and code of ethics are all applied in the game of life. Our aim is to live a spiritual, graceful, compassionate and happy life.

I hope that the articles in this book will guide, inspire and in general be helpful to all of my brothers and sisters on the spiritual path.

The 'essays' in this book are arranged into categories according to the life model that I've formulated and called the Intentional Life Model. However, the articles can be read in any order and used for your daily meditation.

***Figure 1***
***Consciousness & Awareness***
***The Intentional Life Model***

# Consciousness & Awareness

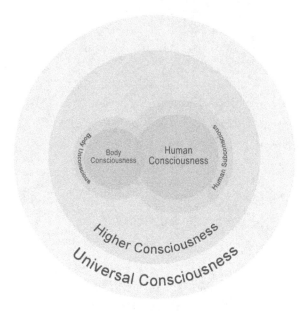

The Human Consciousness Field

---

*Figure 2*
*A Consciousness Model*

Human beings are so much more than we appear on the surface, even to our own minds. We potentially can evolve our conscousness beyond our body and thoughts. We can directly perceive and experience higher dimensions of reality. It is our awareness that can expand beyond our everyday four dimensional sensory framework.

**Awake to Awareness**
**Aware to Higher Consciousness**
**Being Consciousness Now!**

# Overcoming Obstacles to Higher Consciousness

All spiritual seekers have tried meditation and encountered the usual obstructions to maintaining a steady practice such as boredom, daydreaming, increased emotional reactions and even depression. There may appear external obstacles such as health issues, job loss or relationship problems. The stronger the practice the more obstacles appear because a true spiritual path will speed up the karma of a life-time and even access the latent karma from previous life-times.

Of course, one should be aware that not all meditation techniques or systems are best suited to everyone and one of the first solutions is to try different techniques. This however is the most undesirable solution because it is better to make a change when nothing is happening then to make a change because undesirable things are happening. You may consider this absurd because why would we prefer a practice that is obviously causing problems! However, if our goal is to rise to higher consciousness in a short period of time, one should not shy away from growing pains. We will need to work out our karmic ledger in a shorter period of time. Most of it will be taken care of through our practice which should burn away our stored karma. However, there is karma that we have taken into this life and that is now in motion and we can only mitigate, hasten and shorten the effects of their appearance.

The primary solution is to purify the mind by cultivating an indifference to happiness and misery, to pain and pleasure, to all transient opposites. Even what are considered vice or virtue by society are but effervescent plays of the mind and lead to suffering through criticism, gossip, and judgementalism – to be avoided. The true virtues are attitudes of love, compassion, friendliness, joy, gratitude and forgiveness.

Frequently, we are beset by a lack of energy through overwork, family issues, lack of sleep, excessive talking or over-indulgence in the sensory pleasures. It is necessary in such a situation to cultivate the holding of vital energy or prana. A spiritual practice requires a lot of prana to fuel it and if the system doesn't have an inherent technique to increase or acquire more prana, then the student must supplement it by cultivating such pranayama. However, even in a system that has techniques for increasing the vital energy, if the student wastes it on material activities, then progress can be blocked – in such a case, it is necessary to decrease the those activities to a level that does not interfere with the effectiveness of reaching higher consciousness.

When the problem appears to be an unstable or troublesome mind, steadiness of mind needs to be cultivated by focusing on subtle sounds, as well as on the light within. The mere concentration of an external object or even an internal visualization may not be enough to still the mind sufficiently in order to achieve the withdrawal of the senses and in such cases, the meditation on the internal sound of Om can be an effective solution. Also, focusing on light at the third eye center with the appropriate methodology will not only bring about the internalization of the senses and stilling of the mind but can lead to even higher states of consciousness up to and beyond the highest Samadhi that can be described.

Sometimes, it is useful to focus on those sages who are free from attachment – this can also help you acquire a steady mind, especially if you have some past life connection with the sage or can form an effective bridge to the sage in this present life. This can work whether the sage is in the body or working on a higher plane, but is very dependent on the individual seeker's karmic connection and so what works for one may not work for another.

A less common solution but one that may work better for very advanced practitioners is to have the mind be guided from the knowledge derived during the non-waking states. However, this is fraught with danger as more often than not, the ego is involved and the guidance may be faulty and cannot be relied on. Unless the practitioner has already passed through certain tests and been blessed by a Master to have such guidance, then it is necessary to cultivate common sense and discrimination before utilizing the internal guidance to overcome obstacles to higher consciousness.

# Getting the Most of Your Yogic Practice

*Kriya Yoga* teaches that one should make progress and achieve Self-Realization while acting as a householder. This requires not just an outward renunciation of the world, nor the actual retiring to a cave, but an inner renunciation, a non-attachment to the material world. It requires that the *kriya* initiate skillfully lives and works in the world of impermanence and ultimate illusion, deriving the resources necessary to accomplish the spiritual goal of achieving the experience of reality.

An example often cited by the ancient yogis is that of the lotus plant that grows and flowers in the muddy waste-waters, but is not tainted by its surroundings. It remains pure, while absorbing the nutrients from the water and the sun.

In the Bhagavad-Gita, Lord Krishna counsels that we should offer the fruits of our actions to the Divine. In this way, we do not become enmeshed in the results of our actions and are free to do our best without attachment. To expect a reward from our actions is a material way of thinking, while to act selflessly without expectations is the spiritual way of being. Even when we are being paid for our services, we need not be attached to the money, but can offer it to the Divine, to be used to maintain our spiritual life and to help others.

Now, from a practical perspective, how should a spiritually inclined person act?

**The first key to the spiritual life is to set-up and maintain a regular practice or *sadhana*.** Regularity is critical in overcoming inertia and other obstacles to spiritual evolution. A daily practice, preferably once in the morning and once in the evening, no matter how brief, is superior to intermittent efforts performed for hours. This is due to the continual accumulation of negativity that must be overcome before they have the opportunity to take root in the subconscious. Once rooted and supported by existing negative habit patterns, then the effort to eradicate them become ten times more difficult.

Even in mundane matters, we have learnt to brush our teeth everyday – waiting every three days and then brushing for half an hour would seem absurd to our sensibilities. There are those who would brush their teeth after every meal to prevent the build-up of plaque. Take this same enthusiasm into your spiritual life. Perform your *sadhana* regularly and prevent the build-up of negativity and *karma*.

**The second key is to maintain a constant awareness of our spiritual goal.** This awareness is often disrupted by our uneven and irregular life-style. Therefore, it is necessary to examine one's life-style. Take a few moments to note down your daily and weekly activities and examine them. Do you take enough rest, or are you depriving yourself of your health by insufficient sleep? Are you eating healthy food, deriving sufficient life-force or *prana* to remain energetic and positive? It is paradoxical that taking good care of the material body is a mark of spirituality. This does not mean that one should fall into the trap of compulsive dieting, exercising, or absorption in body beautification procedures, which have become part of our consumer culture. However, a consistent asana or postures practice is highly beneficial for the physical and energy bodies.

A healthy body is necessary for spiritual evolution. It is recorded that the great *yogi* Siddhartha Gautama mortified his body through excessive fasting and found that he could not make any further progress in his meditation. Finally, he was so weak that he was dying, rather than evolving, and so he crawled to a stream and bathed himself, ate a small meal, rested and continued his meditation, subsequently achieving enlightenment, becoming the Buddha. He always taught moderation in all things – the middle way.

**The third key is to find a balance between spiritual and material activities**. How much time do you devote to your spiritual life? It is not necessary to spend all your time or even the majority of your time on spiritual activities. However, examine your material activities and determine their necessity. Doing things with your family is necessary and working is necessary to support oneself and one's family. Is working late and taking work home necessary? Is watching television necessary? What is commonly called entertainment is usually an excuse for stimulating a tired mind. Rest and meditation may be a better remedy. Strike a balance.

**The fourth key is to examine the people we associate with - the relationships that we value**. This does not mean that one should give up our long-cherished friendships because they do not involve spiritual activities. It is helpful to cultivate friends who share similar spiritual aspirations and who can provide much needed support. There is a tendency among those new to the spiritual path to try to explain their new beliefs and practices or even attempt to convince close friends to join them. This should be done very delicately and not from a missionary perspective. If one finds that they are not receptive, one should stop annoying them. It is never productive to force your beliefs on others. To keep their friendship, you would need to downplay your spiritual activities. If and when they wish to know more, they will know to ask you. Don't expect understanding and support from even close family members. They fear the unknown and they fear to lose you. Have patience to explain what you are doing – you may have to explain many times, until they see that you are not becoming a fanatic or ignoring them.

**The fifth key is to examine one's work**. Since most of us spend the majority of our day at work, if its performance is a hindrance to our spiritual values, then we need to consider a change. It is possible to work and have provision for financial sustenance without compromising ourselves, or selling our integrity. It is needful to keep in mind the values of truth (*satya*), non-harming of ourselves and others (*ahimsa*) and non-stealing (*asteya*), when examining our work. Another value to keep in mind is our self-actualization – is the work that you are doing utilizing your highest potential? Are you happy in this type of work, or did you stumble or got driven into it? Is this what you want in your life? Consider moving from a high paying but unsatisfying role to a more satisfying position, or moving from a dull low paying job to becoming self-employed.

The possibilities are many, but we need to have confidence in the Divine will. We need to tune in to the Divine and find our *dharma* or right path in this world. When we came into this world, we came with the self-imposed burden of *karma*, but also with the promise of the right path or *dharma* for all of us. By following our *dharma*, we can overcome all our *karma*, and achieve Self-Realization in this life.

Constant awareness of our goal and constant vigilance of our activities will help us steer a spiritual path through the turbulent seas of materiality.

It is a blessing to know that we need and not be enmeshed in what we want. It is a blessing to be satisfied with what we have and not desire what we don't need.

# Remove The Three Faults For Higher Consciousness

Traditionally, when a seeker is accepted into a path of higher consciousness, the spiritual guide begins by giving instructions into the obstacles that prevent the attainment of higher awareness. These are very important but often neglected and forgotten over time and need to be revived every now and then.

It is necessary to continually guard against the three faults as they prevent us from evolving our consciousness and can stunt our spiritual growth.

These three faults are often compared to imperfect vessels. The first fault is that of an upside down vessel – one that is blocked off from further input. It is a reminder to stay receptive. We are often so full of our own ideas and discoveries that we are more interested to tell others about what we think we know rather than be aware of our inherent ignorance and be ready to listen. Let us learn to listen and never stop learning.

The second fault is that of a leaky vessel – one that cannot retain anything. This is an analogy for a seeker who cannot retain the knowledge and wisdom that is being imparted by spiritual guides or even from the books they study. Sincere students need to develop their power of retention – first by paying attention, followed by stronger memory.

The third fault is that of an impure vessel – one that is filled with prejudice, misconceptions and delusions that lead one to misunderstand liberating teachings. Instead of the truth, an impure vessel fills with illusion. The sincere student should strive to remove all such taints that can prevent the pristine perception of reality in the words of those who are imparting the fruits of higher consciousness. Let us all strive to overcome these three faults so that we can maximize our opportunities to learn and achieve higher awareness.

# Overcoming Our Three Mental Defects

Our minds suffer from three primary defects that prevent us from evolving into higher consciousness. Over time, these defects have been called different names and various prescriptions have been given for their removal.

The first defect is called mala which means dirt. This is the inability of one's mind to accurately reflect reality – the mind acts more like a dirty mirror which distorts and clouds what it reflects. This confusion about the nature of reality causes us to be attracted towards external sensory stimuli and becoming enamored of them.

The best antidote to mala is swadhaya, often called self-study. For our purpose, swadhaya is the effort to turn our attention inward and study one's mental processes. There is great resistance and fear to being "alone" with one's mind – that is an affect of mala. The seeker needs to study the appearances and disappearances of thoughts, their nature and source so that she can detach from them. When the seeker no longer identifies with the evervescent thoughts then he has overcome the first mental defect.

However, not everyone can practice swadhaya successfully and an alternative is the practice of self-less work or karma yoga. If one does one's duty without expectations or desires for reward, the mirror of the mind is purified, since it is our desires which continuously muddy up the mirror of our minds.

The second defect of the mind is vikshepa, the fickleness or inability to stay focused. This causes us to move from one attraction to another, one thought to another, without being able to penetrate the thoughts or stabilize them mind. The best antidote is the practice of tapas or austerity. For our purposes, we are talking about the practice of concentration which involves keeping the body still and focusing the mind on a single object or subject. Over time, this will change the nature of the mind and overcome its fickleness.

For those unable to practice tapas, an alternative is puja or japa – ritual worship or the recitation of mantras. These help to control the mind's wandering nature and restrict it to a certain set of thoughts and visuals.

The third defect is the innate ignorance of the mind called avarana. It is the veil that hides our innate nature from our wandering mind. If you think of the mala as affecting our knowledge of the sensory world, then the avarana is affecting our knowledge of our true nature, to access our higher consciousness. Due to avarana, we cannot tune inwards and so tune outwards instead. The antidote to avarana is iswarapranidhana or surrender to the Divine Will. It is the acceptance that there is a veil between our limited consciousness and the wisdom of the Divine. It is the acceptance and cultivation of inspiration and intuition. It is the willingness to let go of our own desires, wishes and even well-being in order to act according to our understanding of the divine will as directed towards the well-fare of others.

By the practice of tapas, swadhaya and iswarprandihana, which the sage Patanjali collectively called Kriya Yoga, one can steady the mind, clean the mental mirror and rent the veil of ignorance.

# Harmony For Higher Consciousness

We are generally not aware that much of Yoga is about harmony. We are in a continual state of disharmony due to our karmic programs and desires – these cause our stress and tension which alienate us from our reality.

Much of the yogic techniques seek to re-unify us to some aspect of our nature which has become alienated.

The practice of yoga asanas harmonize our physical nature within itself – the muscles and tendons with the stretched spine, the left and right side of the body, the front and back, dynamic movement with steadiness and so on. As one progresses with the asana practice, one harmonizes the body with the mind. Ultimately, the goal in the physical body is to unite and harmonize the functions of the two sides of our brain –the cooling right brain and the hot left brain.

We seek to harmonize with our life-force through breath practice or pranayama. We generally breathe in some disturbed and incomplete manner due to our stress and emotions – shallow and quick breaths rather than slow and long breaths. By slow and controlled breathing we are able to harmonize the breath, life-force and mind together. We can reduce stress and lengthen our lives through the proper breathing techniques. The ultimate goal is to balance the left cooling energy channel called ida nadi and the hot cooling energy channel called pingala nadi – this is HaTha Yoga.

The tendency of our senses to turn outwards causes another level of disharmony with our basic nature which can be overcome by deliberately turning or withdrawing our senses inwards with the practice of pratyahara – a concentration at some internal point of focus. When we focus our senses outwards, we expend life-force energy and when we focus inwards, we conserve our life-force energy. This practice balances the external and internal energies.

The process of meditation seeks to find harmony within our disparate thoughts and emotions, to understand the rising and disappearing of thoughts, to merge in the space between thoughts and ultimately to regain our innate awareness. Pen-ultimately, we are seeking to balance our rational and our intuitive minds, while ultimately, we seek to harmonize our soul with our spirit.

Although so far, I've been outlining what is mostly an inward journey, at the same time, we are continuing our sojourn in the world and engaged in the process of self discovery in which we seek to understand and harmonize the various complementary and conflicting aspects of our personality. It is necessary to maintain a certain façade in order to interact with the external world. However, we find that to the extent that the personality is harmonized with our internal reality rather than some fictional set of karmic, social or cultural patterns, we become more and more harmonized with our external reality as well.

There is finally a continual effort to harmonize with others – in our relationships with people around us. Conflicts are continuously being driven by the breakdown of relationships which in turn are due to opposing needs and desires from the personalities of those involved. To the extent that one is able to achieve an inner harmony and peace within oneself, then to that extent, one is able to maintain a peaceful co-existence with others. True mutual harmony arises only when two beings are both able to achieve self-harmony in their nature first and foremost.

Even just thinking about harmony and moving away from conflict is a first step in the journey of self-discovery towards higher consciousness. Let us reflect on how we can bring more harmony into our lives now.

# Open To Higher Consciousness

There are numerous impediments to our accessing higher truths and opening ourselves to the natural states of higher consciousness.

The most devastating hurdle is our innate ignorance. It is difficult to understand what this ignorance actually is and how it operates within us because the operation of our minds are conditioned and controlled by it and so even when we try to figure it out, we are utilizing its surrogates and being handicapped.

In order to better understand ignorance, we can look at what we can consider to be wisdom. In the broadest terms, I would consider wisdom to be the ability to receive, decode and transmit information efficiently and correctly. Ignorance operates to disrupt this process. Conventionally, it is said that wisdom increases with age, but this is actually untrue – what is confused with wisdom is actually the accumulation of experiences and information. In fact, as a person ages, ignorance is reinforced and older persons are generally unable and unwilling to correctly receive, decode or transmit new information wisely. Unfortunately, what used to take many years of ignorant living to produce, has now been compressed into a short time-frame due to the vast communication networks, free distribution of mis-information and faulty mis-education system. I hope this doesn't sound too negative but one has to keep in mind that the culture of ignorance is the normal mode for human society for tens of thousands of years.

Our ability to receive information is impeded by the filters of our prejudices – all of us have been programmed and imprinted with certain modes of bigotries, no matter how free-thinking we consider ourselves to be. It is important for us to actively try to remove these pre-judgements that color our perceptions in order for us to be open to new information.

Our ability to decode and integrate new information is impeded by the filters of our pre-conceptions or reality beliefs. Our beliefs give us tunnel-vision and so we can only perceive a narrow segment of reality but think that we know the whole of it - we need to broaden our awareness of reality and the possibilities in our reality universe.

Our ability to transmit new information is impeded by our editorial and censorship filters. Even when one can receive new information and process it correctly, one can still be inhibited from acknowledging the new world vision and sharing it with others due to its divergence from accepted norms – one can still doubt the reality of one's higher experience and reject the higher consciousness through self-repression. Some may be inhibited due to the fear of repercussions from peer, society or religious institutions. Others may be inhibited due to doubts about the applicability of the higher reality to the general populace – hence, secret societies and elitist approaches. It takes courage to share a new reality to others and it requires a high degree of integration of the experience of higher consciousness to do so appropriately for those struggling with lower consciousness limitations.

It is a long and difficult battle to rid one-self of ignorance operating from one's life-programming, and it is even more liberating when one can rid one-self of the ignorance from our past karma – it is easier to understand that we are limited in our world-view and inheriting our dogmas and prejudices from our life experiences but there is a deeper factor from our past live experiences, which may be more hidden.

Paradoxically, the young child is wiser than the adult because the child is still willing and open to new experiences with less prejudice – the more we stuff ourselves with pre-conceptions, beliefs and dogmas, we lose the ability to expand the scope of our reality. We can become more and more open to higher consciousness as we reject the web of ignorance and open ourselves to the wisdom approach to new information.

# Finding Our True Nature

According to Patanjali, when yoga is achieved with the state of no-mind, then one rests in one's essential state, one's true nature. However, what is that essential state? There is great difficulty in understanding something that cannot be described in our limited mental state but only realized in the yogic consciousness. From ancient times, the acharyas have made many attempts to point towards our true nature.

The following is one attempt to give a glimmer of the mystery of our Self or Atman, which pervades all existence but defy our attempts to isolate it. It is a dialog from the Chandogya Upanishad between Uddalaka and his son Svetaketu.

Svetaketu had already learned all that could be learnt from the experience of the five senses, that is all of apparent reality and his father was now trying to lead him towards that which is beyond appearances:

*Uddalaka said: "Svetaketu! Have you ever asked your teacher for that instruction by which we hear what cannot be heard, by which we perceive that which cannot be perceived and by which we know what cannot be known?"*

*Svetaketu said: "Sir, what is that instruction?"*
*The father replied, "Just as by a single lump of clay, all that is made of clay is known, even so the products of clay being differentiated with separate names does not alter the fact that they are still clay. That is the instruction."*

*Svetaketu: "I don't understand. Please explain further."*
*Uddalaka: "Bring me a fruit from that banyan tree"*
*Svetaketu: "Here it is, revered sir."*

*Uddalaka: "Break it."*
*Svetaketu: "It is broken, revered sir"*
*Uddalaka: "What do you see in it?"*
*Svetaketu: "These seeds, small like particles, revered sir."*
*Uddalaka: "Break one of these seeds, my son."*
*Svetaketu: "It is broken, revered sir."*
*Uddalaka: What do you see in it?"*
*Svetaketu: "Nothing, revered sir."*

*The father said to him, 'Dear boy, this subtle essence which you do not perceive, it is growing from this subtle essence that the large Banyan tree thus stands. Have faith, dear boy."*
*"That Being which is this subtle essence (cause of all), even That all this world has for its Self. That is the truth. That is the Atman. That thou art, O Svetaketu."*

*Svetaketu: "Revered sir, please explain it further to me."*
*Uddalaka: "So be it, dear boy."*
*"Put this salt into water and then come to me in the morning."*
*Svetaketu did as commanded.*
*In the morning, the father said, "Bring the salt, my child, which you put into water at night."*
*Having searched for it, the son did not find it, as it had completely dissolved.*
*The father said, "My child, take a sip from the top of this water. How is it?"*
*The son replied, "It is salt."*
*Uddalaka: "Take a sip from the middle. How is it?"*
*The son replied, "It is salt."*
*Uddalaka: "Take a sip from the bottom. How is it?"*
*The son replied, "It is salt."*
*Uddalaka: "Throw this water away and then come to me'.*
*Svetaketu did so (and returned saying), "It is there always."*

*The father said to him, "Dear boy, as you do not see what is present in this water though indeed it exists in it, similarly, (Being exists) indeed in this body.*

*"That Being which is this subtle essence (cause of all), even That all this world has for its Self. That is the truth. That is the Atman. That thou art, O Svetaketu."*

In the first instruction, the sage was trying to explain how the cause of existence cannot be seen but yet cannot be denied while in the second instruction, he was trying to explain how the spirit pervades all of existence and is not restricted to one place or person, while remaining unseen.

Of course, these illustrations were meant to change the student's world-view and help one penetrate beyond everyday appearances which mask the underlying reality of our true nature. However, they are only pointers and are meant for deeper contemplation by the student to reach an experience of one's true nature which is beyond even the best analogy.

# Mind Your Vritti

A fundamental concept that all spiritual aspirants seeking to understand and control their minds need to know as much about as possible is that of vritti. Sage Patanjali defined that "yoga is the constraint of the vrittis of the mind-stuff."

The vrittis come from the mind, just like the light rays are emitted from the Sun. The mind sends forth a vritti to perceive an object analogous to removing the veil surrounding the object. In order for the mind to perceive an object that it is concentrating on, it must take the form of the object – an image is formed in the mind-stuff or citta. Think how radar is used to detect distant objects and form images of them as the signals are bounced off the objects.

The mind that is focused outward send outward directed vritti or bahirmukha vritti which tends to increase desires and agitation, while during meditation, the mind is focused inward and therefore send inward facing vritti or antarmukha vritti which increases peace and contentment. Remember that there are three principles that underlie all life – the stasis principle, the active principle and light principle – tamas, rajas, and sattva respectively. An outgoing vritti enhances the active principle while an inward vritti enhances the light principle. Meditation results in a sattvic mind while succumbing to emotions and desires result in a rajasic mind.

The desire and attachment to objects is really our desire and attachment to the corresponding vritti in the mind. In fact, due to the operation of our ego, we identify with the vritti of the body – "I am this body," and therefore lose touch with our true nature resulting in suffering and death. We say, "I am afraid," when we identify with the fear vritti and so on and so forth resulting in our binding in this karmic prison. All our emotional ups and downs result from identifying with the vrittis that come and go in the mind-stuff.

One way to further distinguish between vritti is from the source since our mind actually consists of the lower mind or manas based on sensory perception and the higher mind called buddhi. In this way, there is a progression from the manas vritti to the buddhi vritti, from sensory/analytical/error-prone mind function to the intuitive/discriminative/wisdom mind function. Higher still is the witness or sakshi vritti
when the sadhak enters into the witness state of consciousness in which the sakshi vritti enables the witnessing of the modifications of the manas and buddhi. A fourth state is generated when one focuses on one's True Self – this is an undifferentiated vritti of unity. In the fifth stage is the vritti that dissolves all vritti and itself as well and consequently, the mind with it – more than even the worm that eats

it own tail! There are meditations in the wisdom path that teaches how to progress through these five modes.

Another model that is helpful for yogis is that given by Patanjali who also distinguished five vrittis – correct inference (pramana), mistaken inference (viparyaya), fantasy (vikalpa), sleep (nidra) and memory (smriti). These are not all the mental vrittis that one can distinguish but are considered to be the main ones that are critical to control in order to achieve the yogic Samadhi states. The practices of Patanjali yoga suppress these five vrittis in order to rid one of desires and attachment.

There are innumerable vrittis, some strong and others weak and it requires great patience and strength to destroy the vrittis. The practice of yama prescribed by Patanjali – truthfulness, non-violence, turning towards our True Self, non-stealing and non-attachment are fundamental in destroying negative vrittis. The negative vrittis must be destroyed so that the mind is purified in order for the seeker to make progress in higher meditations.

# Know Your Citta

We've discussed the vrittis – the mental fluctuations which inflict our normal state of being. In addition to understanding the vrittis, we must also consider the substratum or ground upon which they manifest, that is, the citta.

The Sanskrit term "citta" is one of those terms that we do not know much about before Patanjali used it in the sutras of his Yoga Darshan and must be understood from that context rather than from later usage. The Vedantists beginning with Shankaracharya seem to have re-interpreted this citta from their philosophical glossary as sub-conscious mind. This can be misleading if we translate verse 2 of the sutras as "Yoga is the cessation of the fluctuations of the sub-conscious mind."

It is clear from the sutras that Patanjali is using citta is an umbrella term for all types of consciousness, not just sub-consciousness. There are therefore various "cittas" and they are all capable of hosting vrittis and moving us away from the state of yoga and so sutra 2 would be: Yoga is the cessation of the fluctuations in Consciousness.

What the in this consciousness? Citta is not one of the tattvas or universal evolutes such as the purusha (spirit / soul) or prakriti (matter) but would be of the material substance rather than a characteristic of the spirit. It is of very subtle matter and seems to have been stimulated into existence by the pususha's interaction with prakriti.

The tattvas which would seem to comprise citta must include manas (the normal mind), ahamkara ("I-ness" or personality) and buddhi (the supernormal mind) – these are all constituents of our consciousness. This rather loose definition makes it possible to distinguish between the citta of someone who is mostly using her buddhi rather than the manas from the citta of someone who has the ahamkara as the primary mode of consciousness.

The constitution of the cittas must also include the subtle substratum which contains the karmic activators or samskaras as well as their active combinations into karmic programs called vasanas. It is these karmic programs which make it possible for the rising and falling of the fluctuations in response to sensory input.

It is sufficient at this time to appreciate the grosser distinctions of citta in order to have clarity in our spiritual practice of yoga. The fluctuations that occur in sub-consciousness, normal consciousness and even super-consciousness must be controlled and stopped by the practice of nirodha (refer to another article in this journal for explanation). Focusing on only one aspect such as the sub-conscious would lead to a state less then that defined by Patanjali.

In the super-conscious states, that is those in dhyana and samadhi, citta is still present and so can be subject to fluctuations. The dhyana cittas are numerous, as are those for the samprajnata samadhi such as the ananda chitta (consciousness of bliss), one level of the samadhi with object. Only when one has gone beyond the asamprajnati samadhi (samadhi without object) and pierced the dharma-megha, does one become free from chitta. Only when one is completely free from chitta can one be completely free – the state of kaivalya.

# Yoga is the State of No-Mind

To understand yoga as expounded by Patanjali, we must also study the Sanskrit term "nirodha" which occurs in the same sutra 2 as the terms citta and vritti.

Now, this nirodha has often been translated variously as restriction, suppression, inhibition and control in the context of sutra 2. These words do not seem to convey the fullness of nirodha to my satisfaction, as they all have certain shades of temporariness and imply that a constant vigilance and/or effort is required to maintain the state of yoga.
It is certainly true that one will need to make the effort and control

the fluctuations of the mind, most notably the thoughts that come and go, in the process of yoga. It is instructive to consider that just as the word yoga is both a process and a state, and while we practice yoga using the techniques of our chosen path, the state of yoga is beyond techniques and practice. The word nirodha is also both process and a state and during the process, control of the vrittis is necessary while the attainment of the state of nirodha would imply the cessation of the effort of control.

It is helpful to look at how the word nirodha is also used by the Lord Buddha before the time of Patanjali – he used it in the sense of extinction as in "dukkha nirodha," the extinction of suffering, one of the noble truths he expounded upon his enlightenment.

It would seem that cessation or extinction is a better fit for sutra 2: "Yoga is the cessation of the fluctuations of consciousness," as it removes the need for constant effort in the attainment of the state of yoga. Although there are significant differences in the usage of certain Sanskrit terms between Maharishi Patanjali and Lord Buddha and it would be erroneous to use the Buddhist meanings in most cases, I think that this is one occasion where it may be more to the point.

According to Patanjali, there are various levels or layers of consciousness or chitta (refer another article in this journal) and consequently there are corresponding levels of nirodha. At the level of the state of dhyana consciousness, the process of control is over the vrittis directly and one can attain to dhyana-nirodha or a no-thought state which leads to the next chitta level of samprajnata samadhi or ecstasy of duality. At this level, no gross thoughts arise but there are abstract forms of thoughts or "presented ideas" called pratyaya and nirodha has to be applied to them.

When pratyaya nirodha is accomplished, one attains to the chitta level of asamprajnati samadhi or non-dual ecstasy at which state, no forms arise but the karmic samskaras or stored impressions appear into our awareness so that we can apply the process of nirodha.

When in the course of time, samskara-nirodha is attained, one is then ready to pierce the cloud of unknowing and experience dharma-megha samadhi in which one can extinguish even the three mighty principles of existence (gunas) – tamas, rajas and sattva and resolve them into their constituents. At this level, one accomplishes sarva-nirodha or complete cessation, a state with no chitta, no-mind or consciousness, but a state of complete awareness in Being.

# Stages of Transformation

In previous articles, we've explored some key concepts from Patanjali in his yogic exposition, such as chitta, vritti, and nirodha. Another fundamental term used by him is that of parinaama or transformation.

Parinaama is a dynamic process and not a specific state of awareness – it is the process of transformation when applied to consciousness that leads to the state of Self-Realization. According to Patanjali, parinaama when applied to the modes of matter, such as the five senses and the five elements will lead to the achievement of siddhis or special powers. In the course of normal activities, parinaama is the change that occurs in all phases of matter, including the accumulation of karmic dispositions called samskaras.

Before we begin discussing the various parinaamas, it is important to point out that these consciousness transformations can only truly occur in the states of samayama and not in normal consciousness. Keep in mind that the three states of dharana (concentration), dhyana (absorption) and samadhi (ecstatic unity) together constitute what is called samayama. The parinaamas are operating on the stored or seed impressions at a deeper level and not on the gross thoughts which have already been dealt with in earlier stages of meditation.

The first transformation is called nirodha parinaama in which the chitta-vrittis become suppressed by expanding the space between mental impressions. When one seed impression disappears and before the next seed impression appears, there is a momentarily gap of no-mind just as when motion in one direction has to be reversed, the object in motion needs to come to a temporary rest first. The transformation occurs when the no-mind gap is extended. The seed impressions are caused by the karmic samskaras and vasanas – the habit patterns and programs from past lives. By the application of effort, a new samskara is built up which aids in the transformation until the gap of nirodha can be extended at will and indefinitely without much resistance.

The second transformation is called samadhi parinaama. The natural tendency during the first parinaama is for the stored impressions to be highly diverse and so we choose a particular object for samayama and it is the form of the object which leads to more focused and specific streams of impressions. In this transformation, the seed impressions are replaced by the essence of the object stripped of its name and form. The mind is transformed into a consciousness of direct cognition of the object – the mind stuff takes the form of the object repeatedly.

The third transformation is called ekagrata parinaama or single-pointed transformation. This occurs when the subsiding seed impression is the same as the arising seed impression. During this transformation, the gap between the arising and disappearing seed impression is expanded to such a degree that the seed impression itself can disappear as if it has been split apart, leading to the seedless or Asamprajnata Samadhi state or the avastha of nirbija.

# The Layers of Mind

Corresponding to the first five chakras or subtle energy centers are five layers of mental function. Knowledge of these five psychological levels is useful for understanding the nature and operation of our bondage to the material world and the means for liberation from this sensual playground. The process of going deeper into our nature and attaining to the True Self is one of expanding our mind to pass through the various levels.

**The first layer is the conscious mind and is the layer of desire:**

There are three functions associated with the first layer – sensory input, feeling either desire or aversion, and acting on the feeling. It is through the five senses of sight, hearing, touch, taste and smell that we receive information about the world. We have the capacity for feeling and the capacity for action through the five motor organs of hands, feet, voice, sexual and excretory organs.

When a young man sees an attractive girl, desire arises and he walks over to her and starts a dialog to satisfy his desire to know her better. After their first date, he takes her to his home to see his collection of spiders. She is immediately repulsed and runs out of the place and develops an aversion to him.

This is the level of instinctual desire and fears – they are quite natural since we developed from animals. As we have evolved, we need to learn to control and channel them.

**The second layer is the subconscious mind – layer for reflection and recollection:**

This is the mental layer that is responsible for most thinking processes – analytical and problem solving of day-to-day life. It is the scientific thought of information management and mathematical computation. This is also where deep philosophical and religious thinking is located. Argumentation arises due to the differences in the sub-conscious minds these thinkers.

This layer holds the function for memory which makes it possible to reflect and think on past experiences and not just on immediate sensory input.

The third function of this layer is dreaming. This is a critical process in order to discharge the excess nervous energy that accumulates in the human body each day. Dreams also help to process our daily experiences or to vicariously satisfy deep desires that do no find fulfillment in our conscious life.

Those who meditate can remove the need for dreams because there is a mental catharsis that occurs in meditation that performs the same function as dreams. The meditator can remain in a deep and dreamless sleep and wake up refreshed.

**The third layer is the super-conscious mind – layer for intuition:**

This is the mental layer of creative insight and is beyond the logic and rationality of the subconscious mind. Many poets and artists have had glimpses of this layer and been raised up from their normal consciousness into the realm of beauty and bliss and have had temporary escape from the anxieties and restlessness of their normal neurotic selves.
This is the layer that is accessed by the greatest scientists such Einstein or Newton and from which their scientific breakthroughs have come.

Deep meditation is necessary in order to reliably and consistently realize this layer of mind.

**The fourth layer is the subliminal mind – layer of discrimination and non-attachment:**

This layer of mind expands our awareness to all the various vibrations of the universe around us, enabling us to perceive the tiniest sub-atomic particle as well as the largest and farthest cosmic structures.

To one in this expanded consciousness, the joys and sorrows, the pleasures and pains of the sensory world are but the plays of a passing show. Such a one who has glimpsed the eternal is un-attached is temporary forms. However, true non-attachment is not a denial of life as some who have not reached this level seems to think. Life in all its changing glory is embraced as a dance of revelation.

Discrimination is the ability to discern the permanent which underlies the changing manifestations of the illusionary world. Realization of the nature of ultimate reality brings to an end all anxiety of loss and fear of death.

**The fifth layer is the subtle causal mind – layer of yearning for union with the Eternal**

This is the final thin veil of the mind, the most expansive layer and yet still separated from our True Self. The separation is so thin that the yearning for unity with the Spirit becomes almost unbearable and intense.

This layer of mind is a radiant golden glow that when directed outwards fills and surrounds the physical body while when directed inwards, it becomes a barrier separating the self from the Self.

The mystics have left us copious testament in their poetry and writings of this great yearning for union with the infinite and unknowable.

The various meditative practices of yoga are formulated to help the sincere seeker realize the different higher levels of the mind and reach the fifth layer. From this layer, persistent and regular practice, together with the grace of the Divine will enable the yogi to pierce the golden sheath enveloping the mind and transcend it.

# Increase Awareness
## *Open To Higher Consciousness*

It is commonly said that 'we should think before we act' but on the spiritual path, the Master says to 'be aware of your thoughts and know the chain of causality before you think or act.'

When we normally start to think about something, we're already lost in our assumptions, biases, likes and dislikes. The "thinking' is merely to justify what we have subconsciously decided to be the best result for oneself.

When one becomes accustomed to meditate by watching one's thoughts without taking charge or changing the direction of the thoughts, one becomes aware of the subconscious motivations.Sit for at least fifteen minutes everyday just ot watch your thoughts.

It might seem daunting at first since we are so used to getting lost in our thoughts that trying to be a watcher of our 'own thoughts' seem a foreign concept. We will have to catch ourselves in mid-thought and detach from the stream of thoughts to watch them.

The practice is worthwhile as it eventually leads one to be less attached to one's own thoughts and to realize the way a thought arises and falls back into the subconscious mind. We might even become aware of the gap between thoughts - this can lead to a momentary bliss of no-thought, no-mind and pure awareness.

Persevere and open yourself to Awareness!

***Figure 3***
***Values***
***The Intentional Life Model***

# The Earth Dream

For the last four hundred years, successive waves of immigrants have made their ways to the shores of USA, in search of what we have since called the American Dream.

In the days of the early settlers, they may have abandoned their European homes because they hungered for religious freedom or perhaps financial freedom as well. Certainly, the "new world" promised them a level of equality that could not be achieved in the more structured societies controlled by an elite of nobilities. It was freedom from unjust taxation that triggered the "Boston Tea Party" demonstrations and ultimately led to the war of independence from the British.

Over the centuries, the financial motive has been a consistent motive for new settlers – the early Chinese immigrants were lured to the "golden mountain" as indentured servants to work on the railroad and other labor intensive programs. In our life-time, it has been the legal immigrants and the illegal migrants from Mexico lured to provide labor for the fields or other non-attractive work. However, whether it was the Dutch, German, Swede, Irish, Polish, Italian, etc., the most enterprising and driven people journeyed here and made "yankee ingenuity" and success the catch-word and envy for the rest of the world.

In the 20th century, the American Dream has been defined as the freedom of the consumer – to be able to purchase whatever you desire. To own one's own home is an aspect of this Dream and unfortunately led to the financial crisis of three years ago. The accumulation of wealth is still an important part of the Dream and this has been responsible for an increase in materialism, if that is possible to imagine. We live in an ultra-materialistic society where everything, including spiritual success is measured in wealth.

Let us switch gear for a moment and up our consciousness to look at why we are here, I mean, why have we been born as human beings on this earth. If we look at the soul as an immigrant, then somewhere in the distant past, we re-located to this earth, to be born here, life-time after lifetime as human beings. We may have started out at something a little less developed as an early mammal or primate, whatever. The fact is that now we inhabit a human body. We had a reason – what dream did we have to come to this earth?

It is certainly true that the human body has developed the capacity for pleasure but there is also the flip-side of pain from accident or sickness. We may have the dream to come for the enjoyment of the senses, but this has not been satisfactory for those of us who have developed their souls to a high degree. These beings whom we call the sages have announced a different dream – the evolution of our consciousness – the capacity of the human body and mind to help evolve the soul to the ultimate freedom of Self-Realization.

If we decide that our initial dream to come to earth was to enjoy ourselves, then certainly the American Dream can be part of this, since we are geared towards the pleasures and comfort and every desire imaginable. However, if we suspect that we came here to find a higher truth, to realize our highest potential, then the current American Dream is not in-line with our soul's Earth Dream and we need to make some adjustment to our version of the American Dream so that it is not at odds with the soul's purpose here. Unfortunately, the mass consciousness is not yet ready to realize this truth and so those who try to live their Soul's Dream will become strangers or aliens in this land of consumerism, of materialism. We can work towards changing the overall consciousness but this will be slow and so those who have realized their true nature and gone on before us have worked to bring about shifts of mass consciousness at different junctures – the next one will be very soon, in 2012, as we have all been anticipating.

However, it is best to keep in mind that the shift in consciousness will help those who are ready for it but may have negative impact on those who resist it. This will actually cause a greater polarity and larger gap between those who live their Soul's Dream and those who want to live the old American Dream. Let us pray for a New American Dream that aligns to a more spiritual purpose.

# Action with Humility

Often in my lectures, I exhort the audience to take no credit for their actions because then they won't have to suffer the negative karmic results or be burdened with the equally binding positive karma. Of course, this is a simplified inspirational message. The reality is more complex.

Karma is an immutable cosmic law that we don't fully understand and have not defined in a rigorous manner. What we have are some hints from the sages who were more intent on laying down guidelines for us to live so that we can avoid future bad karma. For those who wished to be freed from the karmic circle of non-intentional birth and death, they formulated practical spiritual systems such as Yoga.

My words were inspired by the message of Lord Krishna in the yogic classic Bhagavadgita – "one attains Self-realization by doing one's duty with efficiency and without attachment to the results." He further goes on to say that detachment can be attained by, "dedicating all works to me, free from desire and attachment." The result of such practice is - "freedom from the bondage of Karma."

Now, anyone who has ever tried to follow Krishna's counsel sincerely will immediately realize that it isn't easy to be detached from the results of one's actions. We feel elation and pride when the results are positive and we feel remorse or fear when the results are negative. This is just human nature because we identify with our ego and cannot escape from the feeling that we are somehow the actors and fully responsible for our actions.

Only when one is Self-realized and no longer identifies with the body and mind can one truly act without attachment and dedicate all works to the divine. In the meantime, all we can do is pretend, imagine or attempt to be detached. This can be problem if it encourages us to reject responsibility for our actions.

In the process of detachment, the first phase is to actively refuse to take credit for the good that we have done. We need to offer to the divine all the praises that may be heaped on us by well-wishers. Of course, this will not be a perfect act and we cannot help but feel proud but any attempt at true humility will loosen the hold of attachment. Any acknowledgement of the divine actor within us will loosen the hold of the ego.

Naturally, when our actions result in insult or injury and when we are blamed for the consequences, we need to be humble enough to take it and move on. We are still responsible for our actions and need to maintain a level of awareness of the karmic environment. Offer our pain and suffering to the divine actor as well. Will it make us feel better or increase our level of consciousness? Not at the beginning but over time, as our humility becomes more entrenched and automatic, we will understand the law of karma better and be guided more and more by our inner ethical compass (the inner guide).

It is well to keep in mind that the body and mind are always subject to the law of karma. As we strive to attain a higher level of consciousness, we need to follow the ethical guidelines bestowed on us by the ancient sages. A Self-realized yogi does not identify with either the body or mind and so is not affected nor bound by karma but will still function within its limits without violating the universal law. Another way to look at this scenario is that the actions of the Self-realized are always the right one at the right time and so the results have a neutral effect, since he has not acted out of any consideration of good or bad, right or wrong for himself or even others.

For those who are on the spiritual journey and struggling with their fears and desires, there are three paths of actions, the good path, the bad path and the right path. Good or bad is a subjective criteria from the perspective of the un-realized actor – sometimes what one feels is bad for oneself today may be considered good the next day – it is highly variable from person to person and in time. From that person's perspective, the right path may sometimes coincide with the good path which provides no conflict but when it coincides with the bad path then it becomes inconvenient. For the Self-realized, there is only the right path.

# Spiritual Awakening

A sign of spiritual awakening is the dissatisfaction with popular modes of dealing with the meaning of life and the role of humanity in the universe.

The seeker after higher consciousness examines the acceptable ways presented by society to understand the essence of our existence only to find them wanting is some respect or other. This leads to despair until the path is shown that gladdens the heart and illumines the mind.

There have been and still are three traditional ways in the West that sought to understand reality – the paths of religion, philosophy and science. Those who us who try to hide from the mysteries of life and focus on the forgetfulness of desires and "living our lives," try not to think about these paths except in passing or disinterest. Others have tried some variations of these three paths. Some of us merely flirt with them while others commit themselves to one or the other. However, each one way has its benefits and limitations.

Religion starts with the vision of some great soul who tries to communicate his enlightenment to others in their culture but soon becomes a narrowing and exclusive institution run by unenlightened souls who substitute dogma for spiritual experience. Instead of loving all of humanity, religion becomes sectarian and compartmentalized, with its leaders justifying all manners of atrocities by twisting the words of its founder and inventing some new dogma. The genuine seeker who can find so much good and commonality between the words of the great Masters who have given rise to these religions are mystified and horrified by the actual state of their institutions.

Through philosophy, great souls endeavor to understand through their minds the great secrets of human existence in this vast universe. In the past these seekers after the truth have tried to provide answers to others and satisfy their thirst for meaning in life. They engaged in sincere inquiry and honest debate. Although the great philosophers have not been able to formulate one single model of reality that can satisfy everyone, their attempts have yielded all manners of mental heights. Unfortunately, in the last one hundred years, philosophy has become institutionalized and compartmentalized as well, becoming more and more academic, divorced from the concerns of both religion and science. It has become arid, yielding profuse numbers of lackluster academic papers rather than the fruit of a life-long pursuit of truth. It has become a hobby, a university discipline, or a trivial pursuit having little relevance to how one lives one's life.

The material benefits of science have been quite evident from the technological tools and toys that have made life easier, more comfortable and enjoyable. Science has greatly enhanced our understanding of the physical body as well as the physical aspects of our universe, from sub-atomic particles to black holes. However, it cannot provide any answers for those who wish to understand the spiritual life because science has restricted itself to what can be detected by the five senses or instruments which are the extensions of these senses. Before science will consider the spiritual world, it demands that we provide detectable and measurable proof of its existence. Unfortunately, all of science's instruments and tools have been designed for the material world and are not suited for anything non-material. This is like footballers in a football field trying to tell swimmers to demonstrate their skills in the field. Science can only satisfy those who wishes to belief that there is nothing beyond this lifetime and the material world.

Is there another solution for the sincere seeker? We need to consider the way of the East, especially the Masters of India who have always insisted on an integrated path. Only a way that combines the principles of religious devotion to one's higher Self or Divine nature as the goal with scientific methods of experiencing these higher states of consciousness and the appropriate philosophy to support the mental needs of inquiry is satisfying for us.

True Yoga is such an integration of the higher aspects of religion, philosophy and scientific methodology. Without devotion, yoga becomes mechanical and mentally dry. Without philosophy, the mind will wander and doubt such that the practice cannot be sustained over long periods. Without methodical and proven techniques, one merely engages in wishful thinking or emotional hallucinations.

When a seeker rejects a non-integrated path, it is the beginning of discriminative wisdom and an awakening to higher consciousness.

# A Precaution for Meditation

There is a misconception that every system or technique loosely called meditation is equivalent and the same rules apply to them. Most of the time, it is assumed that meditation is always good and can be practiced at any time by anyone with positive results. Such an assumption is incorrect and can lead to unwanted mental effects.

The problem is that meditation is a catch-all word used to describe a variety of spiritual practices and does not really have a strict meaning in English. It can span the simplest concentration exercises to the preliminary mental cleansing methods through to the most advanced techniques that can only be performed in Samadhi states. The common factor is that meditation techniques affect the mind.

The seeker should not meditate when he is in mental or emotional distress. Remember that most meditations require a calm and concentrated mind to begin. When one is not calm for whatever reason, the first thing is to attain a peaceful state before continuing. This can be achieved with mental and emotional healing techniques which can sometimes be also called meditations – these should be the foundation of all meditation systems and must be practiced well before graduating to the higher parts. I've met many seekers who assume that the techniques they have been taught will automatically lead to a calm mind which is usually not the case but they push ahead anyway with the result either that they are too distracted to practice or negative energy infects their meditation.

When the mind is distracted, one waste one's effort – the first priority is to achieve calmness and then concentration. Most meditators have had the experience of distraction and dissatisfaction with their practice. However, less understood is the risk of undermining one's own mind with powerful techniques that embrace the poison of negativity without transforming it. These two cases can be understood from the analogy of physical posture practice. When one is tired but persists in asana practice, one will not have a good experience – either one gives up due to fatigue or one may even get hurt due to carelessness. It is important to rest and relax with gentle movements until one is ready for the postures.

It is good to remind oneself why we are meditating, just as it is important to keep in mind that posture practice is for flexibility and health and not for performance or competition. The prime purpose of meditation is to control the mind. Until some degree of control is achieved, all attempts to engage in higher practices of Mantra, Kundalini or Kriya systems are going to be difficult if not impossible. If one's mind is still in turmoil then one should be careful about the delusions that can arise with advanced techniques.

Always assume an attitude of love and compassion. Give up all fear and anger. Calm the mind. Focus the mind. Then one is ready to meditate.

# The Priorities of Jesus

As we are rushed forward by consumerism to yet another Christmas and therefore the approach of a new year, it is timely to review one of the basic tenets of Lord Jesus's teachings, the beatitudes, and decide whether and how it may affect our actions at the start of a new cycle, whether it is a day, a month, a year or your birthday.

Jesus lifted up his eyes on his disciples and said:

*Blessed are you who are poor for yours is the kingdom of God.*
*Blessed are you who hunger now for you will be filled.*
*Blessed are you that weep now for you shall laugh.*
*Blessed are you when men should hate you, isolate you, blame you,*
*and remove your identity because of me for your reward will be*
*great in the hereafter.*

It is easy to imagine that Jesus is somehow exhorting humanity to abandon their livelihood and duties to follow his teachings in exchange for some future reward after death. It becomes more difficult to interpret this passage from Luke 6 which is called the Sermon on the Plain when it is usually overshadowed by the longer passage in Matthew called Sermon on the Mount which has eight beatitudes.

This passage makes it clearer that Jesus was addressing his twelve disciples especially since in the narrative it is following his choosing of the apostles. Even though he was surrounded by many others who were seeking him for healing, he specifically looked at his close disciples when he gave this teaching. This indicates that the teaching was not for the masses but for sincere spiritual seekers. However, it can be applied to a wider audience if we look at it from the perspective of balancing one's priorities.

It is important to understand that Jesus was not applauding the poor for the sake of their poverty – there many people who are in poverty for many diverse karmic reasons. What is the reason that many sincere spiritual seekers encounter financial difficulties? It is because they've given their priorities to seeking spiritual truths over material benefits. Jesus was stating the fact that his disciples were poor since they'd left their livelihood to follow him and letting them know that they were benefitting in accumulating spiritual wealth. Very few seekers can balance their material needs with their spiritual goals and have financial stability but it is possible and as long as one makes the effort, one has the blessings.

Jesus was not making such a simplistic statement that those who have no food now will have food after death! He was talking about the hunger of his disciples for God, for their true Self, for higher consciousness and for liberation from suffering – it is this hunger that drives the spiritual student to meditate day after day, year after year and to seek after the saints and sages. Jesus was promising his disciples that their hunger for God will be satisfied.

Another characteristic of a sincere spiritual seeker is the grief of separation from her true Self – the isolation of the ego-consciousness from higher consciousness. This grief is another driving force that impels the disciple to move ever forward towards his goal.

The consequence for those who follow the hunger for their own essential Being…for the Truth, is to be reviled by those who are following the material goals of life. We are living in a very materialistic society where there is no allowance for those who are exploring and seeking a different reality than those presented to the masses by those who control the media. The real spiritual seeker becomes an outsider to society.

Of course, it is not my intention to extol poverty due to the searching for God, hunger (even for God), grief from our separation of the Self, or marginalizing by society. However, it is instructive to examine these issues in light of one's current cultural and personal situation. Jesus was addressing his disciples at a particular space and time and we need to extract the lesson from that milieu and apply our perspective.

One lesson that everyone can take heart in is that there is no reason to feel anxiety or shame if one's material life is not as developed as some of our friends and neighbors, as long as you are doing your best in light of balancing the spiritual side of life.

The greatest lesson as far as I'm concerned is that to achieve the goals of realizing the kingdom of God, of satisfying one's spiritual hunger and achieving happiness, one will have to make some adjustment to one's life and re-set our priorities. This is especially timely as we approach a new year, an extremely important year for spiritual progress, that of 2012. For those who are intent on their spiritual goals, an extra effort will yield very high results as I've explained elsewhere. Let's listen to Jesus with our hearts and get our priorities straight for this new pivotal year.

# The Divine Feminine

We just recently celebrated Mother's Day. In this fast moving and non-traditional day and age, it is necessary to remind everyone of the sacrifice and love that makes possible the birth and nurturing of all human beings.

A mother's love is every baby and child's first experience of the world except in the unfortunate cases of orphans (physical or emotional). It is the mother's love or lack there-of that shapes the lives of all human beings. In the Indian spiritual traditions, there is recognition of this power and influence of the mother in the family being reflected in the divine and cosmic scenario.

Even though the Divine in not subject to gender or division, but encompasses all aspects of the universe, it is helpful for mortal beings to envision various aspects and attributes of the Divine so that we can form a connection from our limited perception and understanding to the infinite and unbounded power and consciousness that fills, covers and permeates this universe. For many of us, there is a strong resonance with the feminine mother aspect and this has resulted in the popularity of feminine deities in India.

In most cases, the feminine aspect is complementary to the masculine aspect as in the pairing of the triple divinity. Each of the three primary functions of creation, preservation and transformation is represented by the masculine consciousness of Brahma, Vishnu and Shiva. Each of these is paired with their feminine counterpart representing the power or energy aspect. Brahma is paired with Saraswati, Vishnu with Lakshmi and Shiva with Parvati. It is necessary to consider the pairing more in the nature of two sides of the same coin than to think of them as married couples which many Hindus have the tendency to.

Although there are popular stories about these couples that seem to relate to them as almost human couples in their actions, these should not be taken literally or even philosophically as they are usually meant to teach basic lessons of life using the divine beings as actors in the drama. In the tradition of the sages, the pairs cannot be separated and one side cannot act with the other, just as power without consciousness leads to mindless destruction and consciousness without power leads to non-action.

The development of the Divine Feminine takes on a more unique role in the cosmic drama, because Mother Parvati, the Shakti or feminine power of Lord Shiva, has taken on various other forms for specific transformative functions. These forms have their own attributes and have taken on separate existences with their own associated lore and legends. Such Shaktis include Mother Durga who is fierce in defending her children, the horrifying Kaali Ma who roots out all darkness and negativity from the unverse and Tripura Sundari who is glorious in her protection of creation. Some of the major feminine forms have been grouped together under the umbrella term of the ten Mahavidyas, a primarily tantra tradition.

In the ultimate development of feminine power, the Shakta tradition holds that the supreme Divine power is feminine and all creation, including the triple aspect of creator, preserver and transformer flows only from the One Divine Mother. This extreme homage to the mother aspect resonates with some spiritual aspirants, especially a portion of the tantric tradition and is a legitimate path towards higher consciousness.

Whether you are on one side or the other of the spectrum in perceiving the feminine in the Divine, there can be no seeker who can ignore this aspect. One may need to be reminded that on the yogic level, the potential energy called Kundalini that needs to be awakened and raised for Self-Realization is also called the Shakti or the Divine Feminine. Only when the Shakti Kundalini is raised and united with the Shiva Consciousness in third-eye that Self-Realization is possible.

We need to pay our homage to the Divine Mother as well as to our birth mothers. Our human mothers have given us birth to our human body with the potential for realizing our true nature, while it is Divine Mother who can give us a second birth as Self-Realized beings.

# The Power of Initiation

One of the hallmarks of almost all spiritual traditions is that of the rite of initiation. It is also something that is hardly explained or couched in so much mystery that either one is in awe or one becomes extremely skeptical. In the yogic tradition, initiation is a necessary preliminary to entry on the chosen path of spiritual realization because of the power and protection that it confers on the initiate.

At the most primal level, physical birth is our initiation into the present life – it confers on us all the benefits of being a human being and with it, the protection of our parents and ancestors, as well as the protection of the society in which we are born. When we are initiated into a spiritual tradition, it becomes a second birth – we are re-born and receive the benefits of this new life, together with the protection of the initiator and the lineage of spiritual teachers (living in this or some other plane of existence) in whose names and by whose power the initiation is made.

Why does the initiate need protection? Just life the new-born baby, the initiate is new to the spiritual path and all the wonders and traps that abound on that path. The Masters of the lineage have committed to guide and protect the initiate to overcome those obstacles and to protect her from those who may seek to harm her out of jealousy, spite or inherent darkness.

There are three types of initiations. The first is the initiation into a spiritual organization. The initiate needs to have the aspiration for their higher Self to qualify for this initiation and seek to better himself. The one who initiates has to be a qualified member of the organization and can also act as a mentor or can designate a mentor. The second type is the initiation into a spiritual path and this requires the initiate to commit to sincerely try his best to practice the techniques required on this path for no progress can occur without the regular and persistent effort of the initiate. There are generally different levels of initiations as the practitioner ascents the path. The initiator should be an Acharya or spiritual preceptor who has the authority and power to commit the Masters of the lineage to the guidance and protection of the initiate and who has himself traversed the path and reached the goal.

The third type of initiation is directly into a super-conscious state of awareness. This requires the initiate to have been initiated and achieved certain goals of a spiritual path and is seldom given excepting in the rare cases of high initiates such as world teachers and divine beings with a world mission.

The first type of initiation is very common as it is the model of most religious organizations in which the initiation is called a baptism or sacred thread ceremony.

It is the second type which spiritual seekers are concerned most with since there is a wide variety of simplicity or complexity and requirements for the initiation into a spiritual path. Much depends on the path and the initiator, since an initiation can vary from a simple prayer with or without physical touch to elaborate ceremonies taking hours. The importance should be given to choosing the right path and the right teacher – all else being secondary. The better prepared the initiate, the more profound the effect of the initiation. If the initiate is not as well prepared, results may be slowed but this can be compensated for by persistent practice.

It is recommended that the seeker should not try to make their own way and try to forge their own path without a proper initiation. It would be like trying to climb Mt. Everest without the benefit of any guides or proper equipment or borrowed equipment that they have not learned to use properly. The probability of success is slim at best for such intrepid souls.

# Is Meditation Escapism?

It is tempting especially in times of great upheavals, natural disasters or even personal challenges to try to think about them instead of persevering in one's own spiritual practice. There is a sense of guilt among some spiritual seekers to sit and meditate while there is turmoil about them.

This is a fallacious mode of ego-tripping – literally, the ego is trying to trip us up, because no amount of thinking will solve the world's problems which are due to our own collective ignorance of the true meaning of life and who were are in essence. It is only by the power of meditation that we can perceive and experience reality and bring the bliss and peace from that experience into our daily activity.

Meditation is not an escape from reality but rather the means for reality to be revealed to us. Instead of the erroneous perception of reality due to our limited ego consciousness, we become exposed to the transcendental mode of super-consciousness. A person who has experienced the true nature of divine consciousness becomes fearless in the pursuit of helping her fellow members of humanity and in the betterment of the world. This enlightened spirit in a human body will never lack energy or enthusiasm to help others.

As more people meditate, they become beacons of light and sources of inspiration for the rest of humanity to spur them on to better themselves. When one becomes open to the bliss within, he affects everyone around him in a positive way, radiating peace and calmness in the midst of turbulence.

It is the responsibility of every living being to become a beacon of light by meditating and realizing the reality of their true nature and the nature of reality all around. Therefore, persevere in your meditation in the knowledge that you are not only working towards your own happiness but also helping to solve the world's problems.

# Applying Wisdom in Daily Life

There is a tendency, more pronounced perhaps in the West, of separating how we live our lives from what we have learned from our spiritual studies. Most of the people who study the philosophy or teachings of the yogis and sages, treat them as something interesting to discuss and argue about – they forget that the sages meant their teachings to be lived!

Of course, when one has direct inner experience, one's life will be changed as shown by the stories of the sages. However, without proper knowledge or guidance, the experience cannot be integrated properly and may actually lead to more confusion and greater ignorance. This has been evidenced by the exaggerated and dubious insights of many new-age proponents, especially those who have had near-death or traumatic experiences.

Even a superficial study of the teachings when applied and integrated into our lives can lead to greater peace and contentment. In fact, if one can apply the wisdom of the sages in our daily life, it may actually lead to our experiencing the higher consciousness states from which the sages derived their insights. We do not need to wait until we have our own experience before we change our life-style.

One of the great insights that the sages taught is the transient nature of phenomena and how that should affect our value system. Mentally, we can understand about the shortness of life and inevitability of death, of aging and the loss of youth and vigor, of disease and the loss of well-being. However, emotionally we refuse to accept these truths and this warps our value system, for example, where we try to cover up aging through cosmetic means.

If we know that this body will perish soon, how does that affect our future actions? What do we value and will try to accomplish in the time that we have left? Some may try to accumulate more money or possessions but that cannot be taken with them at death and is futile. Some may try to enjoy themselves to the utmost but even the memories of their enjoyment cannot be taken to the next life.

The sages teach that the only lasting achievement in life is spiritual evolution towards a higher consciousness. Towards that end, we need to balance our work, our family, our enjoyment with our spiritual practice. Should we just abandon our work, family and enjoyment? The work and family are considered to be part of our duty or dharma and abandonment would constitute a running away from our duties which can cause more karmic problems in future lives. Discharging our duties in the best possible way is considered to be a way to work off our karmic debt and is also spiritually evolving. The enjoyment of the senses may be minimized for a time but unless it is totally transformed through a higher state of consciousness, the desire for it will be stronger in the next life.

All spiritual seekers need to perform this balancing act in their lives – sometimes work and family take a bigger focus and then later in life, more and more time may be given over to the spiritual practice. If someone young does not need to work and has no desire for family or sensual enjoyment, then that person through effort in previous life-times has already worked out the proper life-value and may in this life be wholly devoted to the path of spiritual evolution. However, this should be verified by a competent spiritual guide and not be the outcome of deluded ego-desires.

When you next study the teachings of the sages, try to see how their wisdom can be integrated into your life. Don't wait for enlightenment before you make the effort, for that cannot come without an effort to change our values and life-style now.

# The Case Against Ritualism

I've found that rituals can have a positive effect for spiritual practitioners when done properly and for the right reasons. However, it is also true that even something noble when taken to an excess or performed blindly or even for wrong reasons can become detrimental. I'm reminded of this because today marked a celebration of the birth of a yogi saint called Nanak who taught in the 16th century – one of his teachings was to give up external rituals and focus on the internal state of consciousness.

Of course, ritualism in the middle ages had been taken to an extreme in that the focus was all on material gain. In ancient times, each householder performed the proper prescribed rituals for well-being, health, prosperity and spiritual evolution as handed down through the generations. However, due to five hundred years of foreign invasions and occupation, by the 16th century, much knowledge was lost and even simple rituals required the priestly caste to perform and the rest of the population followed blindly. Most of the great spiritual philosophies were forgotten and suppressed. It was in this kind of situation that Nanak found himself.

Nanak saw how the masses were forgetting the Divine and getting mired in rituals out of desperation. He proclaimed, "If they were to know the nature of the Divine, they will realize that all rites and beliefs are futile," and also reminded his listeners of their priorities, "Cursed be the ritual that makes us forget the Beloved Divine."
He advocated a raising of consciousness and mental development instead of following religious prescriptions, "Let compassion be your mosque, faith your prayer carpet and righteousness your holy book. Let modesty be your circumcision and uprightness your fasting. Thus you will become a true devotee of the One God."

Even as child, he seemed to have displayed a similar attitude as shown from the following story – Nanak was brought up as a Hindu and between seven and ten years old, it was customary for a child to be invested with the sacred thread, a symbols of the "twice-born"

– when the priest was called to perform the ceremony, it is said that Nanak refused and spontaneously sang out the following:

*Let mercy be the cotton, contentment the thread,*
*Continence the knot and truth the twist.*
*O, priest! If you have such a sacred thread,*
*Do give it to me – one that doesn't wear out or get soiled.*
*Neither burn nor get lost.*

Whether the story is true or just symbolic, it is true to Nanak's message that instead of focusing on external emblems, or rituals performed by others, or even external rituals performed by one-self, it is better to put one's energy in finding the Divine within oneself. It is better to develop the higher consciousness that encompasses compassion and love for one's fellow travelers on the road than to lavish our attention on things that are transient. It is what is developed in the temple of our hearts that matter.

# Meditation For Wisdom From The Sun

It is recounted in the Mandala Brahmana Upanishad that the great sage Yajnavalkya attained to the sphere of the Sun and learned about the light that exists within the inner core of the spiritual seeker.

The following is the essence of the wisdom imparted to the sage by the Spirit of the Sun:

The human body-mind is burdened with five stains: passion, anger, unrest, fear and sleep. The removal of these stains can is very extremely difficult because it requires the super-human effort to abstain from intention actions, by absolute forgiveness, moderation in food, carefulness and the spiritual vision of building blocks of existence called the tattwas.

There is a subtle path that reveals the mystical star or Taraka which is the way to cross the ocean of suffering where sleep and fear are the serpents of the deep, injury the waves, desire for sensations the whirlpool traps and family entanglements the muddy mire.

Taraka is the Atman when seen in the third-eye center between the eye-brows. It has the nature of the spiritual radiance of Satchitananda. The brilliant central channel, sushumna nadi leads to it and in this channel's center, the kundalini shines like countless lightning bolts and yet is subtle as the thread in the lotus stalk. Darkness and ignorance (tamas) is destroyed there. Through seeing the star, all sins are destroyed.

A technique for attaining the path of the mystical star is given: Close the two ears by the tips of the forefingers, and listen to the booming sound. When the mind is fixed on it, a blue light is seen between the eyes and also in the heart. Deepen the vision and make it steady. When one sees spiritual light above the head, then he attains the state of nectar and rays of the morning sun are joined with the moon and fire in the inner space. Then the yogi comes to have the nature of those lights. Through practice, he becomes one with this inner space (aksaha) devoid of all attributes or gunas.

In the course of practice, akasha, with its shining stars, becomes to him para-akasha and unites with para-akasha. Then she becomes one with the resplendent fire of maha-akasha, Next, she merges into tattva-akasha, lighted with the highest conceivable brightness.

Finally, she becomes one with surya-akasha, brightened by millions of suns. In this way, the yogi becomes one with That.

This is the great yogic science which is concealed in all the scriptures. When this is known, one is liberated.

Then the Spirit of the Sun explained to Yajnavalkya the essence of this inner sight:

It is the source of the five elements. In its midst, the tattvas are manifested. It is hidden. It can be known only by one who has attained wisdom and knowledge. Above the inner sight is the sphere of the sun, in the middle of which is the light of the nectary moon. It shines like a ray of white lightning striking the tip of the nose. When this is practiced, a deep darkness is seen at the root of the palate. In this practice, a jyoti (light) of the form of an endless sphere emerges. This is Brahman as satchitananda. When the mind is absorbed in this naturally produced bliss, then the kechari mudra takes place.

The following are the signs of inner sight: first light is seen like a faraway star; then a dazzling diamond; then the sphere of full moon; then the sphere of the brightness of nine gems; then the sphere of the midday sun – they are seen in this order.

Once the inner sight is attained, there is no rising or setting of the eternal sun of Chit (awareness) in the yogi's heart and he has no karma to perform. Rising above day and night through the annihilation of sound and time he becomes one with Brahman. He is a true knower because he is now free from all thoughts.

When the triple aspects of knower, knowing and knowledge are dissolved by the inner sight, the yogi becomes the jyoti (light) without bhava (existence) or abhava (nonexistence), full and motionless, like the ocean without the tides or like the lamp without the wind.

The yogi who knows Brahman enjoys this bliss, which is eternal and has dawned on her, that yogi becomes one with Brahman. This yogi with inner sight is no longer troubled by the illusion of not-Self, the delusional universe.

This is a glimpse of the wisdom imparted by the Sun to the sage who has reached the realm of the light – the Adityaloka.

# Consciousness through Mindscape

It may be useful for the spiritual seeker if we explore a model of consciousness that I use because it is closely correlated with yogic experience. This model differentiates between brain, mind and consciousness in a practical way for spiritual evolution.

Scientists are still in the process of understanding the functions of the human brain but for our purpose, it is sufficient to use our general knowledge that the brain is a physical organ that collects and processes external stimuli via the five senses. It is also a memory unit storing a record of our physical experiences. The brain is a part of our physical body.

However, in yoga we experience additional "bodies" of subtler material, which we call the energy, emotional, mental and causal bodies, forming a 5-body construct. The mind is a vehicle by which we experience all these bodies. It is not my intention to prove the existence of mind separate from the brain functions – philosophers and neural scientists will be doing that, but to understand it better so that it can be helpful for our spiritual journey.

In this model, the mind is multilevel, from the lowest level dealing with the physical world of the five senses, to higher levels dealing with the reality even beyond the causal level.

At each mind-level the total content of the mind at any moment of time forms the world that can be experienced – what I call the mindscape. That which experiences is called consciousness. The level of one's consciousness is dependent on the level of mindscape that is functioning and can be experienced. The level of consciousness is limited by the mindscape – the total available data and concepts attributed to that particular reality. Ordinary consciousness functions through the lowest human mindscape of the gross physical world of the five senses.

The process of yoga evolves consciousness by enabling it to rise past the different mindscape limitations so that it can experience higher and higher dimensions of realities. At any moment, one's field of consciousness is the mindscape of the mental plane that one is attached to. Each field of consciousness must be mastered before one can proceed to the next. Sometimes, this process can take years and sometimes, it happens rapidly, depending on the overall spiritual practice through many lifetimes leading to a particular moment of time.

At each level of consciousness, we first differentiate all aspects of that particular mindscape. Next, we strive to understand the relationship between the various parts. Then we realize the unity between the various parts of the mindscape. Finally, there arises a realization of one's Self and the mindscape is absorbed – subject and object become one. This four-fold process is repeated at each level of consciousness.

Although one may have experienced higher levels of consciousness, we must reverse back down to the human mindscape to interact with our friends and fellow seekers. It is not possible to provide details of the higher mindscapes due to the limitations of the lower mindscapes – only metaphors and hints can be explored. That is why we must be steadfast in our practice, because an effective spiritual path is the only means to experience the wisdom and reality of higher mindscapes.

# A Strong Single-Minded Desire

## Is The Necessary Motivation On Your Spiritual Path

The worst enemies of a spiritual practitioner are boredom and doubt. Gone are the early heady days when you found your spiritual path and embarked on a set of practice that you were sure would lead you to your goal... you now find excuses to skip your meditation.
To be sure, you have indeed made some progress in steadiness and stability in your life. You may even have a strong sense of peace and serenity. Then you hit a long period of nothing happening. You know you should preserver and keep practicing but it has become mechanical, routine and even boring. You soon come to doubt whether you're even on the right path!

This negative situation happens to almost everyone who has seriously embarked on a spiritual path because of the lifetimes of karmic blocks that we've accumulated and need to be purified or removed – it will take much time and effort. During such lulls between recognizable signs of progress, a lot of work is being done behind the scenes, so to speak and it is imperative not to give in to discouragement.

In order to overcome these periods of boredom and doubt, one should continuously cultivate a strong desire for the goal that motivates us and a set of habit patterns that support our motivation.
Practitioners are confused when I speak about desire for the goal because they've read or heard that we should give up our desires in order to achieve higher consciousness. However, that is a misunderstanding – some wisdom can only be applied at certain stages of the path and does not apply at others. In this case, discarding desire would be like burning a bridge before we get to the other side of the river. We don't need the bridge after we get to the other side but before that, it is essential.

The skillful practitioner should cultivate a strong desire for God, Self-Realization, happiness, bliss, peace or whatever goal can provide the motivation to give your time and energy. It is necessary everyday when you get up in the morning to remind yourself what it is that motivates you. We tend to forget in the restless madness of life. When you sit for your meditation, remind yourself once again why you're doing it.

Another helpful tool is to regularly invigorate and augment the motivation. This is accomplished by a regular habit of seeking out and participating in inspirational forums, such as attending spiritual gatherings especially of those who are Masters on the path. Keeping up with friends who are on the path can also be helpful, as is watching inspirational videos or listening to relevant lectures.

The wisdom and support of others together with your strong desire for the goal will keep you motivated to continue your regular practice, to let your internal wisdom flow unimpeded. When you can connect with your internal guide continuously, you can let go of even the desire as motivation because you'll never be bored or doubtful anymore.

***Figure 4***
***Inspiration***
***The Intentional Life Model***

Rudra Shivananda

# Open the Eyes of Your Soul

Most of us have been so dazzled by the lesser lights of the universe that we have forgotten about the great Light of our True Self – this is the human condition.

We first closed the eyes of our souls in order to enjoy the sensory delights from our physical eyes. Over time, we developed an I-ness or ego-sense which has helped to condition us to keep our soul-eyes closed such that we have lost the ability to open them. We are like blind men and women blundering into each other – we only see the external features but not the true nature.

This brings to mind a parable that you might find interesting:

Imagine a great brilliantly lit hall filled with people who have closed their eyes for so long that they have lost their ability to open them.

They socialized by moving around but since they cannot see, they keep hitting and rubbing against each other, liking some and disliking others; becoming angry at some for hitting them and loving some for kissing them. Sometimes they would knock against a wall or fall down and hurt themselves. Everyone went through times of happiness and suffering.

There were some people at different times in different parts of the room, who managed to open their eyes and see the brilliant light. Once they could see, some looked for the doors, opened them and left the room – they escaped. Some decided to stay in the room and moved around easily avoiding collisions with others. These were enlightened because the light gave them such clarity that they clearly saw everybody around them moving about and all of their misconceptions about what others were actually doing disappeared. They no longer harbored any ill-feelings for someone hitting them. They continued to be hit by some people, but they could better understand what was happening, because they could see.

Some of those with opened eyes started giving guidance to others.

Some gave directions on how to go to less crowded and more pleasant parts of the room – those who followed these directions felt like they were in heaven. Some gave directions on how to open the eyes and those who followed them and made the effort achieved success.

There were those who ignored the importance of opening their own eyes and instead developed fascination and admiration for those with open eyes and started following them blindly. But they got lost while trying to follow, because they could not see. When their enlightened teacher left the room, the followers started arguing about which way to go. Being unable to see, they were all naturally wrong in different ways. Instead of trying to open their eyes, they kept running here and there with closed eyes and arguing with others on where to go. A few determined ones spent a lot time and energy convincing others to walk along with them and felt proud of forming the largest groups and called themselves and religion – a binding together. These large groups would call those who were following different ways and crossed their paths by bad names and even tried to hurt them or even kill them.

Some learned blind folks recognized that various people may have seen the same light though their descriptions were in different words. They realized that everyone will and can see that same light if they opened their eyes. These learned ones identified correctly recognized the closed eyes as the problem. But lacking any practical experience, they grossly underestimated the difficulty in opening their eyes after keeping them closed for too long. They kept telling others that they just had to open your eyes and then there will be brilliant light. A few even imagined that their eyes were open and that they were seeing a bright light.

Some sincere folks recognized the role of effort in opening their eyes and kept trying to pull the eye lids apart consciously every day. However, they had such wild imaginations that together with their desires for experiences that they were carried away and could not focus their energy on actually opening the eyes. They ended up hallucinating that they were seeing brilliant scenes that they had imagined in their dreams.

There were even those who used up their energy on unimportant aspects of the best approach to opening the eyes. They would argue about how to wash the hands before trying to open the eyelids and how much force to use to and what angle to pull them apart. Of course, their eyes remained closed.

Some of them succeeded in opening the eyes a little bit and the flash of brilliant light startled them. Having been in darkness for too long, they could not keep their eyes open for more than a split second. They closed their eyes again, but became proud of their achievement. They assumed that the light could be seen only for a split second by anyone and that they had achieved what the enlightened had talked about. They started erroneous schools of teachings.

Of course, some of them did not complicate things, did not get distracted and tried sincerely using the best method they could think of and managed to open eyes and see light.

I hope you liked this parable which you can add to and develop as I'm sure you can think of a lot of other antics that spiritually blind folks get up to.

# Lyrics for Higher Consciousness

A few days ago, I was listening to an old recording of one of my favorite singers, Edith Piaf. It was the French chanteuse's defining song, recorded in 1960 – "Non, Je ne regrette rien." The sentiments invoked by the lyrics brought me into thinking how some of the popular songs that I used to listen to seemed to tap into a higher state of consciousness.

Some of the lyrics are as follows:

> *No! It all amounts to nothing*
> *No! I don't feel sorry for anything*
> *Not the good things people have done to me*
> *Not the bad things, it's all the same to me.*

To be able to say, "No, I regret nothing" is very inspirational. Most people harbor lots of regrets and it causes mental suffering. We often make decisions that in hind-sight we wish we had not made. This is because we are driven by our desires and fears and not in touch with our inner guide that can provide a basis for making the best decision at any moment. The sages taught that we should use our willpower to restraint ourselves from negative activities and constrain ourselves to the positive path. Most people know what the right action should be but emotional and mental confusion arise due to the desires and fears – this is why we need the ethical and behavioral guidelines which have been taught by the sages and upheld by rulers and leaders of civilization.

However, humanity is now led by leaders and role-models who ignore ethical guidelines and strive to pursue a path of selfishness. In our hearts, we know that such behavior is not in our best interests but it is easier to go with the flow and therefore we are bound with regrets whenever we reflect on our past.

It is not my contention that the lyric writer was necessarily a person of higher consciousness but sometimes creative talents temporarily tap into a higher state and in spite of their original intent, can inspire the mass consciousness. The lyrics serve to remind us, without being irresponsibly defiant, to realize that the past cannot be changed and not to waste energy in trying to re-imagine the past or to harbor guilt feelings that over time will hamper our ability to act in the present. Having no regrets is a state of higher consciousness for one who has strived her best in spite of difficult conditions to live an ethical and productive life. It is not a state of higher consciousness when it is the defiant cry of a criminal or sociopath.

This train of thought brought me to another song that I liked a lot when I was growing up. It was sung in a defining manner by Frank Sinatra, even though the lyrics were penned by Paul Anka:

*I've lived life that's full*
*I travelled each and every highway*
*And more, much more than this*
*I did it my way*

Living in higher consciousness does not lead to an empty life – on the contrary, one should strive to experience all facets of life to the fullest and take all appropriate actions in the course of one's journey. It is not a life of abstention but a life of detached involvement. It is a life of standing up for one's highest ideals and acting in accordance with them. Of course, if one lives a selfish life, then to say, "I did it my way," is not meaningful, but an assertion of immaturity.

In order to give rise to higher consciousness, one should imagine higher ideals that at the moment might seem unrealistic, such as telling the truth or treating one's neighbor as oneself. Let's remember some of the words of John Lennon:

*Imagine all the people living for today*
*Imagine all the people living life in peace*
*Imagine all the people sharing all the world*
*And the world will live as one.*

It is the goal of Yoga to live a full life consistent with the ideals of higher consciousness and act guided by our higher Self, imagining "all the people living in peace," rather than succumbing to our fears and desires. Only such a person can truly sing that "I have no regrets!", that "I've lived life that is full," and "the world will live as one."

# The Attributes of Self-Realization
(inspired by the Upanishads)

The seeker all desires under control
With deep respect the Master approaches
For that direct knowledge of the One Truth
That wisdom light of liberating Self

The divine Guide in grace gives good counsel
Abide in faith and highest devotion
Attain to Self in profound meditation
From soul-mind to Self to God Absolute

Within light effulgence of heart chakra
Discover that transcendent consciousness
In patience and perseverance aspire
Such blessed state to completely immerse

Purify mind, heart, thoughts and emotions
Renounce desires and discipline ego
Meditate on God without distraction
Liberation with Eternal unite

Seated alone in comfort and quiet
Body and back, head and neck, straight to keep
Worldly thought and relationship renounce
Salute with devotion the teacher guide

With calm serenity in heart lotus
That without beginning, middle or end
Realize That One, of wisdom and bliss
Formless, glorious, one with creation

Creator, preserver and destroyer
Imperishable, all-power, all-life
All that is and all that ever shall be
All-love, all-joy, and the death of all-death

Within seven chakras Om meditate
Destroy limitations and ignorance

Know That Self in all and That all in Self
Gain light within, becoming one with God

To express self, Spirit evolved bodies
Each new life molded by old karmic deeds
Discard psycho-physical consciousness
Attain bliss of unity consciousness

From That is born life, mind and five senses
From That is born five great elements
From That is born all the worlds and all souls
Now remember: That thou art; Thou art That

Know That as the object of enjoyment
Know That is the subject, the enjoyer
Know That is the process of enjoyment
Realize That as freedom from bondage

I am independent of the three states
Witness, knower and pure consciousness
Pure, perfect, tranquil and immortal
Eternal, transcendent Shiva, am I

Subtler than the subtle, greater than the great
The universe of manifold forms
The timeless  One of cosmic creation
Eternal, transcendent Shiva, am I

I am the doer with no hands or feet
I need no eyes to see, no ears to hear
I am formless and beyond mind and intellect
Immutable and pure consciousness

All knowledge and wisdom by Self reveal
Self, the revealer of Truth – Self, the Truth
Beyond good, evil, or mind creation
Indestructible, birth-less and formless

In sacred heart, Supreme Self realize
Free from existence and non-existence
Pure and perfect, free from two, three and five
That witness of all, the absolute One.

# To Subdue Body and Mind

Living in Calm and Solitude
Subduing body and his Mind
Within himself in gratitude
Ridding Desires of all Kind.
– from poem Yogi by Yogiraj Siddhanath

It is always instructive to study the words of great Masters, whether past of present in order to keep ourselves on the true path.

This verse is not a call to run off to the hills and caves or give up all social interactions. It is easier to appear to be calm when one is all alone in a cave, but the true test comes when in the midst of interruptions, noise and other disruptive influences, one can keep the calm. Only the calm that comes from being tempered in the forge of the hurly-burly life of a householder can stay the test of time.

The enemy to be subdued is restlessness. The physical body moves and fidgets, the toes tap and the fingers twiddle. The mind is a monkey that runs here and there to get entangled in the scorpion nest of sense desires or climbs up a tree to be eaten by the panther of subconscious impulses. The practice of self-control brings about a steady body and a still mind. The physical body is controlled by maintaining tension-free and steady postures or *asanas*. The mind is controlled by the cultivation of the five restraints or *yamas* – truthfulness, non-harming, turning one's energy towards spirituality, non-stealing and non-attachment to worldly things.

True solitude eludes us because of the dichotomy of body and mind. When body and mind are subdued and they are seen to be only the manifestation of spirit – when body and mind become one with spirit, then true solitude is attained.

As the body and mind become purified, contentment or *santosha* arises. The *karmic* imprints or *samskaras* which give rise to all kinds of desires are then amenable to be removed or burnt off by the fire of the yogi's practice. The very movements in the mind becomes controlled – the vrittis no longer trouble the yogi.

As the layers of ignorance are removed, the yogi lives more and more in his true nature, his true Self. A sense of gratitude to the spiritual guide or Guru and to the Divine arises in the heart of the yogi – not an emotion that comes and goes but a state of Grace that is true devotion or *bhakti*.

# Commencement Address

### *At Self-Realization*

We are now at the start of graduation season and I've been reading about all the ceremonies in the thousands of high schools and hundreds of colleges around the country. Part of the ceremony involves a commencement speech from someone famous or successful in a particular field who is supposed to give some words of advice to the students on their graduation, hopefully words that can be useful as they start a new chapter in their lives. Since many of you are on the spiritual path and are seekers of Self-Realization, I wondered what would the commencement speech from our True-Self be like to a group of graduates who have achieved Self-Realization.

Below is an excerpt from a much longer speech – only those parts which are applicable to the group rather than to each individually (from the perspective of the body, of course):

*My Dear Souls,*

*Congratulations! It's been a long road. You've lived and experienced thousands of life-times and now you have achieved freedom from the bondage of the illusory ego and the delusionary desires of the five senses. You have realized your true nature as the divine and immortal spirit.*

*Through it all, I've been with you day and night. When you shed rivers of tears or enjoyed the peaks of triumph, I watched over you and comforted you as best I could. You did not often hear my words of comfort or guidance but once in a while, the light would shine through. Then one day, you set your heart and sight on me and have since strived and struggled against the current of life to reach your home. It is by your perseverance and self-effort that you have burnt away all your past karma. It is by your meditations that you have reached the state where you no longer act selfishly to accrue new karma.*

*Now, what are you going to do with your freedom? The road to perfection in Being is still ahead, my beloved ones. Some of you will choose to move quickly ahead and to higher planes to perfect yourself. Others may choose to stay on earth and work for the betterment of your brothers and sisters who are still living under the tyranny of the ego and their own desires. Still others may choose the path to return again and again to this plane of existence and perfect yourselves while leading lives of light for the sake of all living beings. Whatever your choice, it will be the will of the Divine. You all have your roles and responsibilities in the divine sphere and some of you will be operating on the cosmic level very soon. It is your will to co-operate with the Divine Will that has set you on your current path and no matter what happens in the future, you will no longer stray from your high states of consciousness which is anchored in Me.*

*I would like to take a moment to remind you that you still have a body to take care of and roles and responsibilities that are a part of who you were. It is proper to reflect on these and seek to act according to the inertial karma which still enlivens your current body from the higher consciousness that you now embrace. You are a liberated soul that still has a physical body shroud.*

*This may be the last time that I will be speaking to you in this manner as we are One and this occasion is merely an artifice for you to remember the experience of duality that you have been suffering for so long.*

*Come, let us embrace our Unity.*

# The Uniqueness Of Ishavasya

There is one ancient text which holds a high position not only because of its lofty philosophical exposition but also due to several unique aspects. The text is called the Ishavasya Upanishad. In the tradition of Upanishads, they all have the common theme of the Atman or the Spirit and its realization. Each Upanishad should also present a method called upasana for realizing the Atman – most times, it is explicitly stated but sometimes only hinted at or made known through oral transmission.

A unique theme of the Ishavasya is that of a personal divinity called Isha. This is a different vision called up by the sage of this text because other Upanishads have concentrated on either the Atman or the Brahman.

The Atman is the true Self – "the form of the Self cannot be seen or grasped by the senses because it is the grasper and seer of everything." It is by abandoning all the false states of consciousness that involve the mind and the senses, that the Self is revealed like the sky when the clouds disappear. Brahman is the term used by the seers to denote the universal, absolute principle that forms the substrate of all beings, divine, semi-divine, human, animal, vegetation, mineral and so on.

The seer of the Ishavasya equates the Atman with the Brahman, the inner Self with the Universal Being. This sage then calls this Divine Being, Isha or Lord, prescribing both a personal and an impersonal aspect to the Divine. This unknown king of yogis has attempted to unite the material with the spiritual by asserting that the Lord Isha permeates the universe and is the Spirit.

The seer then brings together the yogic paths of knowledge and devotion. Traditionally, the followers of the knowledge path would try to directly reach the impersonal Brahman by their intellection and would consider the followers of devotion towards a personal divine aspect as inferiors on the spiritual path. However, our seer points out the merits of both paths and counsels the practice of an integrated path.

In the same grand theme of a uniting vision, the seer brings together the life paths of meditation and action. There is danger in pursuing either one without the other and it is the path of action with awareness that is counseled by the wise. There is danger in devoting one's whole life only to meditation and equally a danger for those who devote their whole life only to activity. A harmonious balance must be sought.

The sage of the Ishavasya tells us further that the Lord will answer our prayers and help us overcome the barriers that prevent us from achieving our Self-Realization. The Lord is not just a dispassionate observer but can get actively involved in our welfare. Such a philosophical position is distinct among the major Upanishads.

The Lord who permeates the universe and is also within us, the seer addresses as Isha. The aspect of the Lord who sustains us is equated with the Spirit behind the visible sun or Surya and is called the nourisher or Pushan. That aspect of the Lord who leads us on the right path is called Agni or the light of the fire.

This text is very short, only eighteen stanzas and is unique in the profundity of its brevity. Most of the other Upanishads explain their visions in much more detail. However, if one can make the effort, one will derive immense benefit from its study.

# Aspiration For The Inner Light

Each human being has an inner Light, but most people do not make contact with their Divinity, even once in their life-time. The physical sun that we observe every-day is very far from our planet. It appears as a small disc, but we know from our science classes, that it is really enormous. Similarly, the inner Light that we have deep within us, seems to be very far from us, and it seems very tiny and insignificant. However, when we approach our inner Light we are illumined and transformed by the transcendental Light of Truth that permeates all existence.

If one is on the path of spirituality, one is bound to see his inner Sun. At first, it might be just a glimpse of it, but the great Masters of Yoga have assured us that if we persevere in our practice, someday will dawn when we will see our inner Sun fully in all its glory. In still higher realizations, we will eventually merge with the Light itself, in Divine Consciousness.

This inner Sun appears to move, which is why the inner light moves and illumines the objects that are sensed by the mind. When it appears to remain still, we enter into silence. That is why in the *Isha Upanishad*, one of the most famous *Upanishads* (an ancient class of spiritual text), we have a description of something that moves and at the same time moves not:

> *That moves and that moves not.*
> *That is far and that is near.*
> *That is within and that is without.*
> Ishavasya Upanishad 5

This is a description of Divinity that permeates the universe and in our solar system is best symbolized by the Sun. This Divinity is the creator that has created something without beginning or end. A great Master once said, "If the beginning comes from anything, then it cannot be a beginning. Beginning cannot come from anything."

In the Rig Veda we learn that existence came from non-existence. Here, non-existence does not signify nothing. It is not something that never existed, it is 'something' which we cannot see with our eyes or detect with our instruments. The seers of the Vedas, through their spiritual sight, through their third-eye, saw non-existence as something which had not yet taken proper form and substance in the outer world.

We all want to bathe in the sea of sunlight. The outer sunlight will give us purification while the inner sunlight will give us illumination. When we want to bathe in water, we need a soap and towel. But when we have a sun-bath, we don't need these things. When we bathe in the inner sun, we need only one thing to satisfy all our inner needs - our soul's communion with our true Self.

The morning Sun comes as the day dawns, and we see beauty all around. God the Beautiful, comes to us in the morning in the form of inspiration. The poet is inspired to write soulful poems, the musician is inspired to compose beautiful music. People going to work from all walks of life, everywhere on this globe, are all getting abundant inspiration from their Inner Light to fulfill their daily duties.

The divine Sun comes to us in midday as dynamic aspiration. We have to perform the duties of the day. We have to fulfill our outer demands as well as our inner demands. The inner Sun comes to us with its fiery flames, giving us powerful, soulful, dynamic will which will hasten our inner evolution and outer manifestation.

The inner Sun comes to us in the evening as realization. When the sun sets, silence and purity reign supreme all around. Nature is resting, Mother Earth is resting and all is peace and love within and without. With evening comes realization, as we offer ourselves for the consummation of the inner and outer fruits of aspiration. When realization dawns and we perceive the inner light directly, the roles of inspiration and aspiration end.

Today we are aspiring, tomorrow we shall be realized. When we are all realized, we shall see that our aspiration and our realization are absolutely inseparable, just as the inner and outer Sun is inseparable.

# The Light That Enlightens

Spiritual practitioners sometimes wonder what it is that is happening when they pursue their sadhana since their true nature is unchangeable and is beyond all actions. What is the effect of their hard work on that which cannot be affected? Why is there a need to persevere in the spiritual practice in order to realize one's true identity when we are already That and only need to remember?
Verse 15 of the Ishavasya Upanishad gives a precise answer:

> *Reality is covered by a golden lid*
> *The practitioner of Truth beholds That;*
> *When unconditioned light removes it.*

This verse describes the penultimate state before final realization, liberation and union with the absolute. It is the summit of our spiritual practice.

As we strive to realize our true nature, we practice spiritual meditations to remove the karmic conditionings of our minds so that we can attain the higher consciousnesses which are beyond the normal sensory mental equipment. However, even in higher consciousness, we are operating in the realm of phenomena, that is, conditioned existence due to the causal chain of duality.

The light of the supermind is still a reflected light that is trapped in the object-subject duality of the manifested universe. There is a barrier that is characterized as a cloud of golden light that envelopes the manifested universe and separates it from the unconditioned and un-manifest absolute reality – paramatma.

Even when we are merged with the manifest light, we are not able to penetrate this barrier. Only when we have removed the most subtle of traces of karma and its potential arising that the unconditioned Light within us is revealed. This is the Light that enlightens for It dissolved the golden barrier that hides our true nature.

Om Tat Sat!

# The Joy Of Tranquility

It is required of the yogic classics to point out the goal of the spiritual discipline, explain the method of practice and the observable result. These three parts usually take up most of the text.

The same three parts are given completely in just one famous verse of the Ishavasya Upanishad which has been quoted ever since by saints and sages for over two thousand years:

*For one who constantly sees*
*everywhere all existence in the Self,*
*And the Self in all beings and forms,*
*Such a one can feel no hatred for anything.*
Verse 6

The goal that is described in this verse is the achievement of Self-Realization and an observable result is the absence of hatred for any "other". The seer has correctly diagnosed the disease as the mental concept of repulsion, dislike, fear and hatred for things in a universe that is comprehended as a multiplicity and plurality of beings similar separate to oneself. There arises in the mind an individual and personal opposition to other beings and objects around us. Such a mind is constantly in stress and overcome with feelings of unhappiness. The mind wavers between the twin blades of repulsion and attraction.

When the mind no longer apprehends the "other" in reality, when the person of wisdom has experienced and realized the Oneness of the Self, then the hatred disappears from the mind. Such a mind becomes tranquil and profound joy arises. As the experience of Oneness becomes more and more established, the tranquility and joy becomes more and more permanent.

The meditation given for achieving this mental tranquility and joy is two-fold.

First, one must practice seeing the Self, the Atman, pervading all existence — animate subjects and inanimate objects. The neighbor who said hello to you this morning, the cat that made a mess on your driveway, the dog that you just walked, the stone that hurt your toe, the air that you breathe, the mosquito that bit you, the bacteria all around and so on, and so on. The Self is everywhere in this country, and all the countries of earth, in the Sun and planets of our solar system, in the solar systems of our milky way galaxy, in the galaxies of our galactic cluster and so on throughout the universe. This is expressed succinctly by the later seers as, "THAT I AM."

As one becomes established in the first mode of apprehension, one moves into the second phase of realization, when one sees One's Self in all beings and forms everywhere. One then experiences that "I" am the neighbor, the drunken driver who smashed into the lamppost outside my house, the tiger in the zoo, the giant redwood and so on and so on. This can best be expressed if that is at all possible as, "I AM THAT."

In one verse, our seer has summed up the work of a life-time, if not for many life-times. Even repeating this verse in its original Sanskrit is considered to bring one closer to the goal, such is its power and lofty vision.

# Outer Space Meditation

The following meditation based on ancient prescriptions from the Upanishads is a useful one to connect with one of the major cosmic building blocks of the universe – the space element or akasha. There are two major ways to connect with the space element, first from an external perspective and second from an internal perspective.

We are sometimes overwhelmed with our personal problems and lose touch with our larger nature. This meditation helps to put things in its proper perspective as we learn to connect with the underlying ground of the dynamic universe and begin to integrate our lower and higher natures.

Method:

1. Sit comfortably and firmly with the least amount of movement. Focus on your breath and let the body be still.

2. After a few minutes, let go of your breath and become aware of the still body again. Let your awareness float to the top of the head and look down on your face, the front, back, left side, and right side of the still body. Look at the clothes you are wearing.

3. Next, float to the ceiling of your room and become aware of your position in the room, as well as the rest of the room's contents. Look at the door and the windows.

4. Rise higher still above your house. If necessary, feel your awareness being connected to the body a golden thread of light. View the different rooms in your house and the furniture in them.

5. As you rise higher still, you become aware of the town or city – the streets, the buildings and parks.

6. Now, move your awareness to an orbital level around the earth and become aware of the continent your city is on and the surrounding seas. Let the earth rotate and view all the continents and oceans.

7. Let the earth become smaller and smaller as you move further away until the solar system is just a star among many of the milky-way galaxy. As you move further and further, even the galaxies become tiny lights within the void of space. Become aware of the space all around you. Become one with the space but still separate through you awareness. Rest in this state.

8. Slowly, become aware of the galaxies around you and move towards our galaxy. Become aware of our solar system and move into orbit around the earth with its continents and blue oceans. Descend to your city and then to the house and back above your head. View your still body and examine it while you slowly become aware of the physical body once more – the head, the neck, the arms, torso and legs. Slowly move a hand and turn your head slightly, taking long, deep breaths and open your eyes.

# Maya Angelou – Courageous Soul Consciousness

A poet, writer, society spokesperson and fearless crusader are some of the images evoked by Maya Angelou, who recently passed away. I would also like to highlight her role as an evolved spiritual seeker who can give guidance to others seeking to rise above the waves of a turbulent life. Her tremendous child-hood adversity and trauma strengthened rather weaken her resolve to improve herself – in spite of the fact that many poor souls have been destroyed by similar experiences.

What I admire about Maya most is her unblinking honesty and steadfast grasp of the truth, powered by her admirable courage. She has often highlighted the need for courage in life as the single most important virtue:

> *"One isn't necessary born with courage but one is born with potential.*
> *Without courage, we cannot practice any other virtue with consistency.*
> *We can't be kind, true, merciful, generous, or honest."*

In tantric yoga, it is said that in order to lead a spiritual life in a dark age, it is necessary to cultivate *vira-bhava* or courage. When one reads Maya's autobiographical books, there is no denying that she exemplified the heroic virtue in her life.

In yoga, we teach that events happen to us and around us due to past actions or karma and that we are not usually able to change the environment, but we can act with our will towards a positive reaction instead and improve the situation rather than react negatively. In a similar vein, Maya has said, *"You may not control all the events that happen to you but you can decide not to be reduced by them."*

We are always counseling spiritual seekers to be careful about what kind of experiences they attract – the music they listen to, the food they eat, the friends they associate with, the books they read and so forth, because these can affect their minds and cause new karmic affects. From her own hard-won life experiences, Maya counsels, *"You are the sum total of everything you've ever seen, heard, eaten, smelled, been told, forgot – it's all there. Everything influences each of us and because of that, I try to make sure my experiences are positive."*

All the great saints and sages have lauded the virtue of love, whether in the highest abstract sense of in the grossest passionate sense, love conquers negativity and should be cultivated to the fullest extent. In Touched By An Angel, Maya has written:

> *We, unaccustomed to courage*
> *exiles from delight*
> *live coiled in shells of loneliness*
> *until love leaves its high holy temple*
> *and comes into our sight*
> *to liberate us into life.*

It seems to me that Maya Angelou has shown that she has made use of her life, learned important lessons and is worthy to be a beacon of light to other seekers. I say this not because she was famous – that is a by-product of her courage and soul force, but by the fragrance of her life, a life well-lived. Death has not extinguished Maya Angelou's light – she will continue to shine through her words to guide generations of troubled souls.

# Let us Pray for Mahatma Francis

Yoga is not a religion. It is an experiential movement towards higher states of consciousness. Yoga is more of a way of being and living than about beliefs or practices. Yoga is about personal experience and not about scriptures or the teachings of others.

Yoga is not a philosophy. There are many different "philosophies" within the Indian framework that have been applied to the way and state of yoga. From Samkhya to Advaita to Kashmiri Saivism, yogis have used what could help to explain their experiences to those sincere seekers who aspired to the spiritual life. However, these philosophies were not ends to themselves, but only means to satisfy inquisitive minds so that the seekers could eventually get their own experiences indicated.

Two thousand years ago, Lord Jesus walked the earth and expressed the way of love and inclusion. He renounced the way of dogma and exclusivity that was propounded by the ruling priestly caste. He lived his life in accordance with his teachings – he truly walked his talk. His catholic or universal way formed the foundation of a movement that later solidified into a religion.

The current leader of the catholic movement attributed to Lord Jesus recently visited USA and there was much hype and adoration as well as controversy. Whether one agrees with the beliefs and dogmas of the modern version of the catholic religion, one must take a moment to consider the words and actions of Father Francis.

A yogi is an embodiment of the experience of Self-Realization, of higher consciousness. A yogi's actions reflect his or her higher state, free from dogma or influence of others. A yogi walks his or her talk. One who is well on the path of the yoga of action and service is a mahatma or great soul.

From the moment that Francis took up the office of the papacy, he brought a fresh breeze to an old institution. He has been trying to bring back the pastoral nature of the office – to be a shepherd indeed to his flock.

What impresses first are his words – direct and straight from his many years of working with his flock. His words of wisdom and humility can be found all over the web now – I would encourage you to check them out. His words are of comfort, seeking to embrace the different and diverse members of his church, rather than to condemn or punish.

What continue to impress are his actions which have for the most part matched his words. He has renounced the ostentatious life-style of some of those who have occupied his office in the past. He has slowly passed measures to bring the marginalized back to the fold. He is focused on those that need the most help – the poor and hopeless – those ostracized because of life-style choices or genetics. He is truly a wise and humble soul dedicated to the service of his flock. Such a being at the top of a religious organization is extremely rare. This is surely a divine grace at this time.

Of course, as a person, Francis is still limited by his circumstances and beliefs – he is not free of dogma. In spite of these limitations, he is making a great effort to shift the course of his titanic institution back towards the true way of the Lord Jesus – the way of love and inclusivity. Let us pray for this great soul, Father Francis, that he be given the time to bring forth some of the reforms that he is striving for. May Francis become a yogi of Christ - to be unified in Christ consciousness.

# Spiritual Guidance from Martin Luther King

A few days ago, we commemorated the life of a great leader for the freedom movement. Martin Luther King took up the mantle of Mahatma Gandhi and became a beacon of light not only for black Americans but for people all over the world. We need not discuss his heroic application of the principles of non-violence to restore the civil and human rights of a marginalized segment of the population because it is well-known and applauded by all unbiased peoples of the world.

However, I've always been impressed by his spiritual foundation and the wisdom of his words when applied to a yogic setting. It's not that there is any lack of wisdom in the yogic literature or the words of the yogic Masters, but when someone from a different tradition shows his wisdom not only in words but his skillful deeds, then one must take notice.

Although I was not in the states at that time, MLK became a spiritual inspiration to me when he became the most prominent civil rights leader and his speeches were reported in newspapers that I read. It seemed to me that he actually walked his talk and his life and works were an application of his principles which were rotted in deep spiritual truths. I'm not familiar with his mode of prayer or meditation, but his strong faith shone through his words and actions. His were not the words of a philosopher but held practical significance because they came through his experience and that is what yoga is about – yoga is about personal experience.

Yoga does not stop when one has achieved higher consciousness - Yoga is about applying one's higher consciousness to solve life's challenges and to help others mired in darkness.

I took a small sample of the quotes [bolded and italicized] that were being tweeted about and chose the following to illustrate how his words can be applied to help yogic practitioners.

**"Peace is more precious than diamonds or gold"**
A great strength flows through spiritual seekers when they establish the correct value reference in their lives. Although we must live and support ourselves in this material world, we should not fall into the trap of making money or possessions the center of our existence. We should always keep an eye on our goal of personal and world peace so that we can prioritize our sadhana or spiritual practice over transient or frivolous desires.

**"If this [peace] is to be achieved, man must evolve for all human conflicts a method which rejects revenge, aggression and retaliation. The foundation of such a method is love."**
Love and non-violence are the keys to applied spirituality. It is not sufficient to mouth mere platitudes in our meditations if there is no difference in our actions towards others. The goal of applied yoga is to evolve our consciousness to a higher level so that we are no longer ruled by our lower instincts but guided by the experience of the unity of all beings. The development of love and non-violence is also critical to achieving higher consciousness because if our actions reflect negative attitudes, then we accumulate bad karma which become obstacles to yogic progress!

**"Forgiveness is not an occasional act, it is a constant attitude"**
When we have peace in our minds and love in our hearts, we can forgive others for their misbehavior. If we engage in the negative karma of tit for tat, the greatest hurt is done to ourselves and to all of humanity. If we hold on to the negative emotions of anger or hurt, we lose our peace of mind and we cannot meditate.

**"Life's most persistent and urgent question is 'what are your doing for others?'"**
It is not enough that we forgive others, we need to take positive action to help those mired in the darkness of their ignorance and are committing negative karmic acts. Of course, as seekers, we need to develop an attitude of compassion in order to be able to act in accordance with the universal law.

*[87]*

*"Darkness cannot drive out darkness, only light can do that.*
*Hate cannot drive out hate, only love can do that"*

The power of yoga is to increase the light in our consciousness – yogis are filled with light and devoid of darkness. Decreasing negativity and increasing love helps to increase light in our lives and helps to integrate meditation into our everyday actions.

*"The time is always right to do what is right"*

Spiritual seekers are always wondering when they should do their practice – it is very clear – any time and any place is the right time and right place, rather than trying to find the perfect time or place. Of course, we counsel regularity and give guidance about the best times, but life is not always obliging and students procrastinate at the slightest doubt.

*"Faith is taking the first step even when you don't see the whole staircase"*

You must have faith in your chosen practice and path to preserve in reaching success on the spiritual path. Remove doubts and replace with faith based on the teachings of the Masters.

*"This faith can give us courage to face the uncertainties of the future. It will give our tired feet new strength as we continue to our forward stride towards the city of freedom."*

Have faith in your chosen practice and take courage to overcome your doubts about the fruits of meditation which sometimes seem to elude you or take so much time to make their appearance. Don't give up – when you persevere, you will find the strength to overcome all your obstacles to reach the ultimate freedom of Self-Realization.

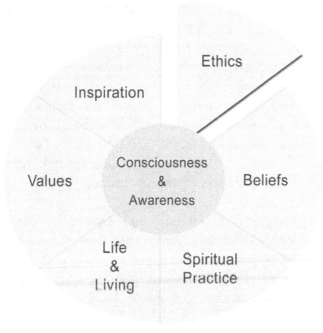

***Figure 5***
***Ethics***
***The Intentional Life Model***

# Tame the Wild Beasts

One of the myriad names of the Divine is the Lord of Beasts – Pashupati, which is usually considered to indicate the Lord of created beings. However, from the internal perspective, wild animals are the internal emotions, uncontrolled desires and passions which ravage our peace of mind and an important part of attaining higher consciousness is to tame these wild beasts, becoming in a microcosmic sense, a lord of beasts ourselves.

We possess a menagerie, a veritable zoo within our minds – the lions of pride, the wolves of hunger, boar of lusts, the bison of ignorance, deer that run in fear and so on, as far as our imagination can reach. On the other hand, we also are aware of the emblems of domesticated animals such as the bull that attends the Lord or the lambs that came to witness the birth of a Jesus – these tame animals represent our human nature rising above our animal nature.

Higher consciousness is about rising above the animal consciousness to the human consciousness and staying in the human consciousness – this can only happen when the lower wild animal nature is tamed. Moreover, higher consciousness is about rising above even the human consciousness to the level of Divine consciousness – a superhuman feat.

In the first phase, to tame the wild beasts, we need to apply self-control. In our society of excesses and consumerism, self-control is thrown out the window – the popular society encourages a level of letting go – from over-eating to over-sexing, from over-acquiring to over-emoting. Self-control is confused with repression in pop psychology and discouraged – accordingly, it is better to let out some steam than control the anger.

In most spiritual traditions, it has always been recognized that controlling one's thoughts, emotions, speech and actions are the first steps in attaining the goal of higher consciousness. In yogic traditions, we have narrowed it down to no more than five areas for self-control:

1.      Tell the truth and don't lie – this includes living your truth as well – walking the talk, so to speak!

2.      Refrain from harming other living beings – this includes looking after your own well-being also.

3.      Refrain from wasting your life's energy on non-essential activities – you can enjoy yourself but not over-indulge.

4.      Refrain from stealing – this includes taking credit for the work of others.

5.      Do not be attached to things – all things are transient.

The sages have determined that if we practice these five rules, we can tame the wild animals. For instance, we lie or harm others because of fear or desire to gain something, or because of pride and so refraining from lying or harming others control the animal passions of fear, desire and pride. As we look forward towards celebrating the birth of Jesus, let us consider the rules of self-control that we may tame our animal nature and eventually have our own Christmas day.

# Does the End Justify the Means?

Recently, during some news analyst program, the journalists were decrying the dishonesty of one of the major political parties in their spoken and unspoken lies being spread to bolster their position with the electorate. They basically proved that these political leaders were knowingly misrepresenting lies as truth because the lies evoke strong emotional responses from their supporters and may lead them to win in upcoming elections. This kind of activity seemed to be in-line with the philosophy that the end justifies the means – whatever it takes to win seems to be encouraged in the current American way. In another program, one political leader was asked whether he agreed with some outrageous position being spouted by one of their candidates – that unemployment benefits was unconstitutional, and responded by saying that, "he agreed with whatever it takes to win the election."

It is not only in politics but we have seen it in our business leaders before and after the current economic crisis, in sports and in our education system. It seems that something is only "bad" if one is stupid or careless enough to get caught at it, in which case, one deserves to have the book thrown at one. In every aspect of our lives, there is a relativistic concept that a lie is as good or sometimes even better than the truth – whatever it takes to achieve a certain result.

There are many ways to approach this question, from moral, ethical, religious, or philosophical terms, but I would like discuss it from the perspective of the yogic spiritual law of karma.

Now, there may be three aspects of an action from the karmic perspective – the intent of the actor, the act itself and the results of the act. It seems from study of the relevant authority that intent seems to play a very small part in the karmic impact. We need to actually analyze the act and its results to get any insight. What we call the "means" could be a series of acts and "the end" may only be one desirable result from a series of consequences from an act. For instance, a desirable goal may be the winning of a war, but this may entail the result that millions of people may be killed and millions others suffer various hardships. The Law of Karma does not forget about the unintended consequences or the unavoidable side-effects.

There are certain acts that have been deemed a-priori harmful from a karmic perspective – they will always cause a negative karmic effect on the actor. Such are acts such as lying, harming others, stealing, etc. These are based on the accumulated wisdom and insight of past sages. So in order to accumulate good karma and avoid bad karma, one would tell the truth. In fact, it would go beyond that, since it actually mandates that one would need to make an effort to ascertain the truth because it is not enough that one thinks one is telling the truth when one is actually wrong.

It is actually easier to agree on acts that should be avoided such as murder than it is to agree on which "ends" are good or bad. In fact, it may not be possible because of so many conflicting human desires and needs – for instance, nobody would object to peace but what if your leaders tell you that it takes a war to get peace. Is this war an end or a means? While Karl Marx was concerned with the economic and political equality of the masses, he was not concerned with the proper means to achieve such equality and humanity has paid a steep price. A freedom fighter wants to achieve freedom for his people and employs terror tactics – is this justifiable?

Let us look at a simple situation. Would you lie to save the life of another person? One may be justified to say that the bad karma from lying would be outweighed by the good karma of saving a life, and one would probably be right. However, what if the person whose life was saved turned out to be a Hitler and caused the deaths of millions of innocents? Then the negative karma from the act of kindness would be very great indeed. This helps to point out a flaw in our human condition – we are incapable of being able to foresee the many consequences of even our simplest actions! This does not mean that we should then be frozen in inaction and agonize over even the simplest decision to eat or not to eat something. However, it should give us pause to examine our fallibility and this in turn should lead us to conclude that we cannot try to juggle or justify whichever means to achieve our desired ends.

If we can agree that certain acts are a-priori negative, then we should avoid those acts, regardless of whatever desired results may be achieved. This will restore to us the ability to act, without a constant consideration and balancing of possible consequences. Does this mean that we would not be subject to bad karma? Not necessarily, but it is the best that a human consciousness can achieve. If one can become a Buddha, then one can foresee all the consequences of an act and the complete karmic results, but that is beyond our scope at this time.

I'm not saying that war is never justified because it involves killing which is a-priori a negative act, but I'm saying that those who start a war, no matter how justified they think it is, should be ready to take the heavy karmic burden. Sometimes, it doesn't take long to figure out that a particular war turned out badly even for the winning side – that the situation that one country's leaders wanted to achieve, such as greater security or chance of world peace, was not achieved and instead, one evil was removed that enabled a greater evil to grow unchecked.

Every action has its consequences and to think that the karmic effects of a series of actions will somehow be offset by a desired objective is delusionary. One should strive to achieve one's goals through the least harmful means and if that is not possible, then one should re-examine the goal and its desirability. If one still persists in achieving a desirable goal in spite of the possible negative acts, then one should be ready to take the karmic burden with courage.

Somehow, I don't think that winning an election, a game or passing an exam is worth the hurt that unethical and harmful means will generate. It is only the illusionary hope that one can get away with it, that one would not be caught or that the immediate consequences of being found out would be negligible that power the ascendance of "the end justifies the means" in our society. We must try to remove this ignorance with education about the universal law of karma.

# The Moral Imbalance

I often come across seekers on the spiritual path who are struggling with the situation of their lives. Most of them are not aware that they are engaged in the advanced practices that cause the speeding up of karmic issues. The disruptions in their lives are a side-effect of the yogic techniques. Unfortunately, most of them are not prepared for the eruption of these issues and become depressed or give up their practices. A few, even turn negative and let their suppressed subconscious programs take charge. This deplorable situation is due to the Western tendency to take short-cuts and to bypass the foundation practices that have been given by the past Eastern Masters.

In ancient times the sages emphasized the development and practice of ethics above all as the pre-eminent spiritual practice. However, in present times this has become unfashionable and there is much greater emphasize on the Guru's grace or in the effectiveness of techniques. It is understandable because the effect of grace or the techniques are more apparent while that of morality is difficult to ascertain from our worldly perspective.

However, there is great harm in neglecting the development of moral character as part of one's spiritual practice.

Effective spiritual practices which lead to self-realization have to release the past karmas so that they can be either worked out positively or removed by further practice. However, such a release usually gives rise to emotional or mental reactions that can cause new karmic consequences. For example, memories of past traumas can give rise to emotions such as anger or despair and if one cannot detach from such emotions, they will be expressed outwardly against another person, thereby causing new negative karma. In this example, the spiritual practice, rather than help in progressing towards less karma would increase one's karmic burden instead – a step backward.

When you are firmly grounded in positive virtues such as truthfulness and harmlessness, then you can easily process all the "stuff" that come out from your practice without being negatively effected. Rather than an emotional catharsis which causes more emotional ripples around, you would be able to release the negativity by detachment or transformation.

Transforming a negative emotion such as anger into a positive emotion such as love takes practice and does not happen automatically. That is the reason why we must form ethical habits and the moral injunctions such as those given by Patanjali in his Yoga Sutras are a reminder that they are necessary. Living life under these ethical rules helps to generate the behavior patterns that will enable us to deal with the unfolding of our karmic burdens successfully. From a subtle perspective, our nadis and chakras are purified through the practice of the ethical rules so that the chakras can be awakened.

The training in ethical living leads to a moral character that is pure in thought, word and actions. A seeker who has developed this moral purity should not be confused with the religious bigots who claim such a status. A person of pure mind has developed her sattvic or lightening character and interacts with others from a perspective of non-judgemental love. Such a person accepts others as they are and helps all who seek help. Such a person has studied their own psyche and accepts their own totality without letting the negativity take control. Such a person develops a consciousness of contentment and accepts all that live can give. Such a person is suitable to practice advanced yogic techniques because they cannot be disrupted from their purity and contentment.

Of course, I've sketched an ideal situation but we don't always have the opportunity to attain such ethical, pure and contented consciousness before embarking on advanced spiritual practice. I've found when talking with those who are currently suffering through their karmic issues, that just knowing that it is happening because of their own practice and that it is ultimately good since it will lessen their karmic burden, has in some ways helped them.

There is still time to consider the importance of ethical rules in your spiritual life – it will smooth out a lot of the negative events and help you cope better. We cannot control what is happening around and to us, but we can control how we react to these events..

# The Foundation of Yoga

In what is considered one of the definitive texts of Yoga, an eightfold or ashtanga process is defined, from self-restraint (yama) to unity consciousness (samadhi).

It is instructive for us to understand why the yogic sage Patanjali has placed ahimsa (non-violence) as the first of the yama. Non-violence is the most important practice to perform – it leads to the perfection of love. It is the most practical to practice because it is very easy to observe whether one has broken the self-restraint in action, speech or thought. The perfection of love removes the veil of duality and ignorance, merging into satya or truth – the highest aspect of which is the realization of the essential one-ness of all Being. With the perfection of satya, all covetousness is removed and non-stealing or asteya happens in due course. The ultimate in stealing is the thought of keeping something away from the Divine, the giver and owner of all there is. With the perfection of asteya, all that we have is offered to the Divine, which is what brahmacharya is all about – the turning of all our energies toward the Divine. When we have given our all back to the Source of All, what is there to be attached to anymore? The perfection of brahmacharya leads effortlessly to the practice of aparigraha or non-attachment.

Although the five restraints in the yamas is given as a progression, one leading to the next in perfection, this does not mean that the spiritual seeker needs to wait for the perfection of one before practicing the next. They should all be practiced in unison as a completely integrated way of life. However, each cannot be perfected until the previous one has been perfected first, and therefore ahimsa is the most important one to work towards.

When the yamas are perfected, there is an emergence of saucha o rpurity, the first of the niyamas (higher virtues). The purpose of the self-restraints is to provide the ground for purity and by perfecting purity, all thoughts, words and deeds become sanctified and will no longer incur new karmic consequences. With the perfection of purity, contentment or santosha arises in consequence. You might now start to wonder how contentment could possibly lead to austerity.

It is well to recall that tapas (austerity) is actually the development of inner fire, and this inner fire requires the quenching of all desires, which can only occur when contentment is perfected. When the inner fire has developed by burning all the desires, it is then possible to realize one's true Self, and svadhyaya (self-discovery) becomes a reality. With the perfection of svadhyaya, one can truly surrender to the will of the Divine and practice the perfection of ishvar pranidhana.

Again, the niyamas are a natural progression from the yamas, and each niyama smoothly merges into the next.

The third anga of Ashtanga Yoga, after niyama, is asana (steady posture) because when one has perfected the niymas, one has control over one's physical body and can achieve a steady posture for deep meditation.

The fourth anga is pranayama, the control and expansion of the life-force energy. This pranayama is a practice of combining the tapas or building of inner fire, done with self-awareness of svadhyaya and with devotion to the Divine, in a state of ishvar pranidhana. By the continuous and prolonged practice of pranayama, the state of pratyahara or the internalization of the senses comes about. It is important to remember that pratyahara is the consequence of the consistent practice of life-force control. The deepening of pratyahara leads to dharana or one-pointed concentration, which leads to dhyana or meditative awareness, which leads to samadhi, states of blissful absorption into the Self and eventually the Divine. Each limb of Ashtanga Yoga flowers into the next, as opening blossoms encouraging the growth of the next higher lotus bloom.

From the perspective of understanding the perfection of these eight aspects of Yoga, they are like the steps on a ladder leading from our current state to the yogic state of Self-Realization. You have to go from one step to the next. However, from a practical or constructive model, these eight parts are like the spoke of a wheel and we need to practice them according to the yogic system that we are engaged in.

Yoga is not possible without the fragrance of the yama and niyama, that is their purifying and transformative power – they are the foundation of Yoga. Let us firmly make our progress on the spiritual path by building the strong foundation of self-restraint and self-discipline for higher virtues..

# Remedy For Obsessive Behavior?

Every now and then, a spiritual practitioner will contact me and reveal that he is struggling with an addiction to on-line pornography and ask about remedies. After a little research, it appears that this kind of condition is not uncommon with the proliferation of on-line sites in recent years. In a short article, I can only briefly touch on some ideas that I feel are the most important to share.

There is no easy answer to the cause for the rise of such obsessive behavior because there can be a variety of karmic factors involved with the human sex drive. Every one of us is now inundated with sexually vibrant advertising on a daily basis and this can trigger many samskaras (karmic patterns) from past lives of unfulfilled sexual desires. Most of us will try to suppress them but without a firm spiritual practice to remove the samskaras, they still lie dormant waiting for the right environment to manifest.

There are those who may think that obsession with pornography is a harmless issue. Even if it does not result in directly harming someone else, it can be harmful for the one obsessed. A lot of energy is wasted in pursuit of their compulsion and this can be detrimental to their work, their relationships and even spiritual practice.

It is generally not a good idea to try to sort out the complex causal chains that have led to the current problematic behavior pattern. The least useful advice generally is to use your willpower to stop because if that were possible, it would already be done – ask the smoker, the drinker etc. to stop and we know what happens. The best remedy is to devote one-self to a powerful spiritual practice such as Kriya Yoga which can remove the fundamental causes of all negative behavior. However, normal spiritual practice takes a long time to counteract such compulsions in those without a very strong will.

Another remedy, possibly swifter, is to embrace the tantric philosophy of inclusion. However, be warned that this is a sword-edged path fraught with great dangers. On this path, all aspects of one's self are accepted without condemnation. Accordingly, guilt is actually the greatest detriment. However, this is not a license for negative or hurtful behavior as some have tried to put into practice. The more enlightened Tantric utilizes meditation to fulfill their desires and will incorporate the pornographic material. The essential difference between the meditation and indulging in sexual fantasy is the stated purpose – one is to extricate oneself from delusion by going through it while the other is to enjoy it. Eventually, the practitioner would be able to view the pornography without be effected by it, physically, emotionally or mentally.

The first step to deal with a compulsive behavior is to recognize that it is a problem. Then one should seek help – from a support group or program if such exists for the negative issue. Keep in mind though, that, such 12 step programs etc. are not a cure, but an effective means of coping with the problem. Only a spiritual remedy can eliminate the root cause.

In the case of the on-line pornography, most of those over 40 years old seems to be suffering from guilt while those in their 20s not so much. The older ones seem to understand that the activities shown in pornography are not reflective of the loving relationship with a partner while those younger have difficulty in discriminating between cultural norms and pornographic hyperbole. This can be very dangerous in the case of violent pornography which seems to be on the rise.

Whether a spiritual person with the pornographic obsession chooses to continue with what may be a harmless pursuit or seek a remedy through some form of spiritual practice, the key to decrease any possible future harmful karma is to commit to moral restraint. It is important to behave in accordance to the spiritual guidance of the Masters – positive conduct with respect for all living beings. This is the guiding light of truth that can help the sincere seeker overcome such obstacles as compulsive behavior. Always remember the first rule of karma – Do No Harm to others or to oneself.

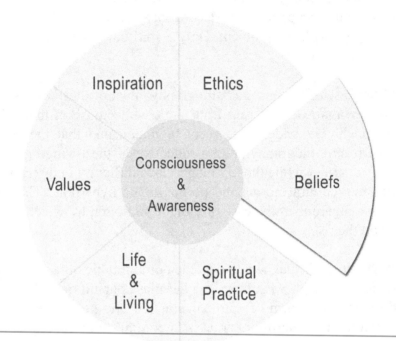

***Figure 6***
***Beliefs***
***The Intentional Life Model***

# Don't Blame Divine Will

Recently I received an email from a spiritual seeker who had been initiated into Kriya Yoga. She wrote that after practicing for about two weeks she developed a nasty flu that made it impossible for her to do her sadhana for the last 6 weeks. Although she is now recovered, she feels that she will abandon her practice because it must be divine will that she stop Kriya - that the flu was a sign!

Although most people have not developed sufficiently to intuit Divine Will when necessary, these same people will not hesitate to ascribe to the inscrutable workings of this divine will any odd happenings that might support their own subconscious desires or fears. This mysterious divine will is used to support any decision to start or stop certain activities without regard to common sense or spiritual insight.

The ego is ever on the alert for opportunities to defeat any threatening activities such as spiritual practice – it is necessary to persevere in the face of such fears.

There are many reasons why seemingly negative events occur in one's life – most often it is in some way the workings of the law of karma – there is a cause relationship between what is happening now to something that one has done in the past. If Divine Will has anything to do with it, it would be at the level of the setting up of this universal law of karma and not at the specific level causing an event to occur. The spiritual seeker should understand that it is her own karma that is being worked out during the flu season and there is not really a sign to stop her spiritual practice.

However, this is not to say that the spiritual practice had nothing to do with the karmic flu surfacing. It is true that one's practice can accelerate the working out of karmic issues – this is necessarily so since the karmic burden one has undertaken to work out in this specific life-time cannot be removed without any outward effect. The karma one is working out in this life-time is called prarabdha karma and will be accelerated by spiritual practice. It is possible to lighten the effects through the practice but not to entirely eliminate them. One must realize that the practice is eliminating that larger portion of karma that is called sanchita karma or the unripened / stored karma that would take effect in some other life-time.

If one stops one's practice because of karmic effects in this life-time, one will be doomed to suffer the karmic effects in future life-times. However, if one perseveres in this life-time, then there is the possibility to remove future suffering completely or at least to some degree.

It is also important to keep in mind if one were to embark on an enterprise to help others such as a clinic for the poor of a particular place, there may be many obstacles that can come due to the karmic blocks from the population to be helped. This is not an indication to give up because one expects that if the divine wishes it to happen, it will come smoothly!

We do not know the will of the Divine, but we can be guided to do the right thing at the right time. However, even if we are acting according to the Divine Will, there may be many obstacles that need to be overcome – we still need to persevere and make our best effort and leave the result of success or failure up to the Divine.

# A New Approach In Education Is Needed

There are inherent flaws in the current education system that has persisted for several hundred years because of a lack in the understanding of human nature. John Locke in the 17th century epitomizes this ignorance when he stated, "I think I may say that of all the men we meet with, nine parts of ten are what they are good or evil, useful or not, by their education."

The basic beliefs underlying our education system can be summarized as follows:

1.      The child's mind is an empty cabinet or tabula rasa (blank slate) and education is about filling the cabinet with "correct or useful" teachings

2.      It is education which determines the well-being and usefulness of the person since the child is born inherently good but can get messed up due to a bad environment

3.      Child-hood impressions are the strongest and we should ensure that there is as much positive input as possible and not find fault with the child

The problem is that in reality, the human consciousness is only one-tenth of our nature and nine-tenths are hidden in the subconscious mind. None of our education systems are trying to address this vast uncharted territory. According to the yogic sages, we are not born with a blank slate but with the burden of karmic imprints due to our past actions – we are born with "programs" which pre-dispose us to certain emotional and mental reactions. The flaw in our education system is that we don't even try to teach any system of ethics to overcome the negative pull of our subconscious mind. Ethics is somehow confused with religion in the West and so there is no pursuit of proper behavior in a secular environment. In religious schools, the position is to throw guilt and fear at the child in order to control the negative tendencies, further alienating and confusing the human potential.

There is no easy solution to the current mis-education as there are no teachers who can actually provide the needed therapy for overcoming karmic imprints in grade and high school environments. It is necessary to educate adults who can in due time take over the roles of teachers in our school system. A top-down approach is needed. There is a need to formulate a yogic system of education which recognizes the role of karmic imprints and can overcome these imprints so that the teacher can be role models for future generations. Currently, our teachers in school are for the most part well-meaning and hardworking but blind to the real problems troubling their students. The students are not being educated to realize their human potential.

We will first have to train a new generation of adults who can become responsible parents and teachers. Each one needs to be instilled with an ethical compass and provided tools to handle sub-conscious imprints, without which he is just a puppet dancing to the strings of his programs. Can this be done in one or two generations? Probably not, but I sense that a start will be made soon to go the next step in human education. In the last one hundred years there have been spiritual people who have tried in various ways to setup better educational systems but these have been isolated and have had little impact on the general education system controlled by governments.

It will be necessary to utilize the wisdom of the yogis and sages within the context of the modern world and to make it relevant to the peoples of our times without burdening everyone with the need to overcome all suffering and attain liberation, for not everyone is seeking release from this world. It is necessary to provide the means for increasing human consciousness in the practical context of being a better person and attaining more freedom of expression in positive ways. My Master says that human beings must evolve from "man the brute to man the Man and then to man the God." The current education system is deficient in evolving us to our full humanity because it does not recognize the fundamental reality of karma.

# Problems with a Materialistic Philosophy

It is sad that the prevalent philosophy among the majority of humanity is one of materialism in some form or the other. Even among those who profess spirituality, there is in reality a desire for some subtle form of material gratification. There is actually a profound danger in the material view of the meaning of life that is quickly causing a degeneration of the value of an individual to society.

What do I mean by a materialistic philosophy?

It is easy to understand the traditional material philosophy which reasonably maintains that all that exists is apprehended by the five senses and their instrumental extensions – it is all matter and there is no proof for anything that is non-material. It finds support in science and in fact science now assumes that the universe is only matter and no longer even tries to look on any alternative view except to suppress it with orthodoxy. We are also familiar with political systems based on material philosophy such as communism and how they have affected human freedom and creativity.

What may not be so apparent is the religious materialism that underlies much of the major religious institutions in the world. Even though they are based on the philosophy that there is more to humanity than the physical body and that life extends beyond death in some form or other, in practice they emphasis material success and elevate the rich and powerful beyond the holy. Religious institutions are based on materialism even though their raison-d'etre is the spiritual welfare of its members. Many crimes against humanity have been perpetrated by these religious institutions through directly instigating wars mass persecutions or indirectly by propaganda programming of its members.

Most insidious is the often neglected spiritual materialism which poisons the efforts of many sincere spiritual seekers. This is very common in India as well where spiritual techniques have been subordinated for the gratification of material needs, whether possessions, wealth, relationships, job advancement or better health. This is not to say that one cannot be spiritual and can still satisfy material needs, it is the danger of spending spiritual energy and efforts to acquire material gains that is to be avoided. I shall go more in depth on this subject in the future. It is easy to consider a prime example – the perversion of yoga postures and the very name of yoga for the purpose of fitness and figure in "yoga studios" throughout the world. Don't get me wrong, I have nothing against exercising and keeping fit and admire the teachers who help in this manner, but what I object to is the hijacking of yoga postures solely for this purpose and forgetting about the true purpose of these postures as a base for yoga meditation.

Actually I'm only mentioning these other types of materialism because it would be unfair for you to think that the problem is only with scientific materialism. We need to uncover the undermining of individual freedom that is being caused by the scientific philosophy because it is this that has more open as well as hidden and subconscious influence these days then religious or spiritual materialism.

Let us consider what popular science is understood to tell us – human beings are just the result of a series of accidental and random joining of proteins evolving over a period of time through natural selection on an insignificant dust-ball in a non-remarkable solar-system within a mediocre galaxy, one among countless billions of them. Everything concerning a human being can be understood by knowing about the material interaction of some form or other – no non-material mind or soul exists. When an individual human dies, that is the total end of that individual's existence – there is nothing beyond death.

Since the general population has a great faith in the conclusions of science in terms of physics and cosmos, biology and medicine, chemistry, engineering and even the pseudo-science of psychology – we are so in awe of the technology that has produced so much improvement in the wellbeing and life-style of humanity that we would accept what science is saying about the metaphysical subjects such as soul and re-incarnation that it has not made any serious attempt to penetrate or understand better.

Serious thinkers who accept scientific materialism have grappled with the dilemma of motivating humanity towards a set of non-spiritually induced ethical behavior. How do you get people to behave well towards each other if there are no consequences in the after-life or in a future life? Focus is then on the betterment of humanity – in scientific materialism, the individual is insignificant, only the perpetuation and betterment of humanity is important. This means that the individual should be sacrificed for the well-being of the many. This kind of thinking is being used to justify all sorts of laws and regulations which take away individual dignity and freedom.

In scientific materialism there is no necessity for individual evolution, no transcending of individual limitations, no Self-realization or liberation from the cycle of birth and death. Such efforts would be meaningless. There is no respect for the individual apart from his or her contribution to humanity. True spirituality actually looks at things from the opposite side – humanity exists for the sake of the individual – this is because every person is potentially divine and can attain to higher consciousness. For spirituality, every individual is precious as each one is a receptacle of the spirit – each body is the temple of the divine, capable of evolving to unimaginable heights beyond the dreams of science, philosophy or religion.

It is important in this time to re-affirm the importance of the individual, not to the detriment of everyone, but with a balance of fundamental rights and not let fear-mongers justify the throttling of freedom in a country that has prided itself on being the country of the free. We respect the province of science but it should also know its limits and not be used to justify a materialistic philosophy. It is important to realize that science has not proven the non-existence of a spiritual reality but merely limited itself to the material world and can neither affirm nor deny the spiritual. There is no conflict between real science and real spirituality just as there is no conflict between physics and biology as long as each recognizes its scope and limitations.

# Learning About The Self

Once upon a time, there were two students who approached the Master for instruction into the nature of the True Self. They had been told that knowledge of the Self gives one knowledge of all things and were eager to master the universe.

The Master accepted these two students and they served him and were disciplined by him for twelve years. At the end of this period, the students approached their Guru and asked for the initiation into the nature of the Self.

The Master replied, "Go and look into a pan of water and what you see is the Self."

When they looked, they saw their own face and body. The first student jumped up with joy and proclaimed that the body is the Self. He thanked the Master and took his leave and returned to his homeland to teach his revelation – that the only reality is the material world and therefore, one should seek all types of enjoyment of the flesh. He became famous and many came to him from all over the world to learn this truth.

The second student pondered on the revelation and had a doubt because he had been taught that the Self was immortal but the body ages, sickens and dies. He again approached the Master and asked for further instruction.

After another six years, he approached the Master for the answer. The Sage said, "What you see in dream - that is the Self." The disciple sat and pondered for a while and rejected this also as dreams were only reflections of the waking state and their appearances were transitory and not permanent.

He asked to stay for another three years, after which he again approached the Master for the truth. The Master then said, "What you see in the state of deep sleep, that is the Self." The disciple reflected deeply for some time and once more rejected this as deep sleep was experienced as darkness and nothingness and brought no revelation.

The Master asked his disciple to yet stay another three years at the end of which, he would impart the wisdom sought. With folded hands and empty mind, the disciple once more approached the ancient One and asked for initiation.

The Master smiled and placed his hands on the disciple's head in blessing and an immediate realization of the truth blossomed. The disciple realized his Self was not the body that decays and dies, nor yet the mind that sleeps and gives rise to transitory dreams. Yet after the darkness of deep sleep, there is still a continuous identity on waking – an unchanging Existence, a Being that is beyond body and mind – unaffected by the experience of pain, aging, sickness, sorrow and death.

At that moment, he became aware and realized all transitory experiences and changing states as ripples of mind matter dependent on the ground of Consciousness. It was utterly beyond words or thoughts – indescribable, only realizable. He understood why the truth of the Self could not be imparted by the mind to another mind. Finally, he was aware of deep Bliss as the wisdom of the universe was revealed to him.

He who was the disciple realized that the Self is Existence, Consciousness and Bliss – Sat Chid Ananda.

He touched the feet of his Master and both embraced. No word was spoken as the awakened One departed to spread the truth of the Self to those ready to experience it.

# Misconceptions about Yoga

Whenever I talk to someone about my devotion to Yoga, I wind up having to explain that it is not what has been popularized in the media. Yoga is not really about physical postures and is really a spiritual discipline for Self-realization. Of course, there is no doubt that the Hatha Yoga asanas (postures) do provide a good system for keeping the physical body healthy, flexible and coordinated with the mind. It is the ubiquitous equating of asana practice with Yoga that is requiring a lot of energy to overcome and can be an obstacle for those spiritually inclined to explore the transforming aspects of this ancient discipline.

Imagine my amazement when, on a recent visit to Hong Kong I read in the South China Morning Post a sensational article purporting to be about yoga. The author, who has a doctorate in physics but makes no claims to any study or knowledge of Yoga or even asana practice, based all of his statements on an article in the New York Times. Apparently, the founder of Anusara Yoga was embroiled in a sexual scandal and had been forced to resign. This seems to have provided the pretext to launch a series of misinformation about Yoga as a whole.

The first piece of misinformation was that ancient Yoga was about enhancing sexual satisfaction. This is patently erroneous because the authoritative work on classical Yoga is Patanjali's Yoga Sutras authored over two thousand years ago. In this text, the sage maps out the evolution of higher consciousness. There is no mention or hint of sex. The eightfold aspects of the yogic system and the various states of higher consciousness formulated by this sage have over time been adopted in various ways into many non-yogic philosophies. The definition of Yoga laid down by Patanjali is "the cessation of the modifications or perturbations in the mind." Controlling the mind and the senses and going into meditative states called Samadhi is the hallmark of Yoga.

The second misinformation in the article was that Hatha Yoga is the basis of all systems of yogas. Since Hatha Yoga is of recent origin – only about one thousand years old, this is of necessity erroneous. However, since all western styles of yoga are concerning postures with some breathing techniques, it is understandable why someone might commit this error. Hatha Yoga is most associated with the practices.

The third misconception is that Hatha Yoga is of tantric origin. A casual study may lead to this confusion since modern tantras do employ Hatha Yoga techniques, but this is of a more recent amalgamation. It is not the case that Hatha Yoga utilizes tantric practices or philosophy. I'm sure all of you are aware that the term Tantra is used to loosely convey the aura of sexual pre-occupation. It is beyond the scope of this article to try to clarify the deeper and original spiritual context of Tantra. My intention here is only to indicate that Tantra and Yoga are different disciplines.

The authoritative text for Hatha Yoga is the aptly named Hatha Yoga Pradipika which states very clearly that it is the first half of the classical Yoga and is the foundation for the subsequent practice called Raja Yoga. In essence, Hatha Yoga is comprised of the first five steps of Patanjali's eight step system. These are yama or body/mind restraint, niyama or body/mind development, asanas (physical postures), pranayama (life-force control) and pratyahara (sense-withdrawal.) The remaining three steps of dharana (concentration), dhyana (absorption) and Samadhi (unity consciousness) is collectively called Raja Yoga. The practice of pratyahara is the bridge between the two. Therefore, Hatha Yoga is an integral part, together with Raja Yoga, of a practical system developed utilizing Patanjali's framework. It is not derived from Tantra.

The increasing burden caused by both Western and even Eastern misconceptions about Yoga is reaching an alarming pace. I sincerely pray that we will not have to pay the price of abandoning the use of the term Yoga due to the heavy misuse and prejudice.

# The Existence of the Soul

There is a fascination among Western spiritual people to speculate about the existence of God, even though no-one has ever succeeded in proving either that God exists or that God does not exist. Simply, the definition of God is beyond the scope of our logic and mental boundaries. However, closer to home, a question that all sincere seekers should make an effort to ascertain is whether their souls exist and its relationship with reality.

Even the existence of the soul seems to be beyond our current scope of scientific research, just as X-rays would have been to the budding scientists of the 17th century. How else can we approach the soul if we cannot measure it, weigh it, photograph it or write an equation about it? The truth is that we need the soul to exist if there is to be any sense in our search for the true Self… if we have any existence beyond this lifetime.

Even though there doesn't seem to be any proof for its existence, most everyone is convinced that they have a soul. We feel that we have a continuous existence that transcends the body and mind – we take it for granted and although we don't know what it is and how to take care of it, we get worried once in a while about its fate when the body and mind dies. In the west, the concern is whether the soul will go to heaven or hell, whereas in the east, the concern is on the next re-incarnated state.

Even a book would be insufficient to deal with the vast subject of the soul and so we can only touch upon that aspect which is germane as far as Self-realization is concerned, which is the very nature of the soul according to the sages of yogic wisdom. The soul is called the jiva and is neither eternal nor unchanging – it is the capacity of the soul-jiva to evolve that is of greatest interest to all sincere spiritual seekers.

It is the existence of this soul-jiva that is the cause of human suffering because it is only the apparent self — the self that is subject to karma and is re-born over and over again. The soul-jiva is hypnotized by the ego and enmeshed by the five senses. The soul-jiva has taken up a relative existence in matter. However, the soul-jiva is only a reflection, albeit a sentient reflection of the soul-atma which is spirit, eternal and unchanging. It is the soul-atma that is the true Self.

This is somewhat analogous to the hypothetical situation when a character in a role playing video-game has so disengaged itself from the actual player that it seems to have a mind of its own and engages in the game without the active participation of the player who only watches and may sometimes give some guidance! The character is still subject to the rules of the game and cannot "see or know" beyond its limitations. Of course, this analogy breaks down quite easily but it does give a sense to the human dilemma as far as the soul-jiva and soul-atma is concerned.

The process of yogic awakening and in fact for all spiritual awakening is the progressive expansion of the consciousness or awareness of the soul-jiva until it realizes it is really One with the soul-atma. At this stage, the soul-jiva gives up its apparent existence and there is only the soul-atma – this is the dissolution of the apparent self and the realization of the True-Self, which has never been enmeshed in matter, and which is spirit.

# Destiny and Free-Will

There is a constant friction in the minds of truth seekers when it comes to whether there is pre-destination or whether we can determine our own fates. This is natural because although we would like to believe that we have the freedom to choose our paths, more often than not, our experience is that things just happen and we feel powerless to make the changes that we might aspire to.

People seem to be drawn to the same situations and make the same mistakes over and over again. This is because of our habit patterns and the imprints that have accumulated in this present lifetime as well as from previous births. Even if you don't believe in re-incarnation and past lives, a little examination will confirm all the childhood and teenage imprints from parents, relatives, teachers, friends and enemies, as well as from the rigid norms of society.

What are these imprints? They are the automatic reaction complexes which have been set up in our mental and emotional minds. They are the programs that make us wince at certain situations or words and laugh at others. They are the prejudices that make us avoid certain people and places and attract us to some others. We hardly give any thoughts to the thoughts and emotions that are triggered by advertisements, political rhetoric or our favorite songs. However, what goes well in one part of the country or with some ethnic groups will not work with others. The programs are different. The common factor is the lack of freedom.

We are proud to salute the flag that symbolizes that we are the land of the free, but most of us have not made any effort to free ourselves from our programs. We do not think, speak or act freely but under the control of our programs which force and limit our response whether we are aware of it or not. Some become aware of their imprints but feel helpless to do anything about them. Others think that by rebelling against their parents and society will make them free – this is an illusion as found out by the hippies in the 60's. The change must be internal, not external, through removing the imprints and not through drugs or bizarre behavior.

The practice of yoga is to attain freedom from our imprints and to be able to think, speak and act freely.

The innate sense of suffering and unhappiness that humanity feels is because of the lack of this freedom, without which, we find ourselves trapped in the wheel of destiny. However, destiny happens only because we follow our programs. If we act according to these imprints, it is like we are following a well-tread path and not deviating from it – of course, this means that it is easy to predict where one will end up!

Humanity has been obsessed with mapping our destiny, whether from the stars, the palms, the face or tea-leaves, entrails, bones, numbers or geometric figures. The staggering amounts of effort put into these endeavors indicate that there is a certain predictability to our lives.

However, it is also taught that we have free-will. However, this elusive free-will is an illusion because even our choices in the food we eat and the clothes we wear are determined by our imprints. Why does one have this favorite color and not that one? A myriad of other why's that we never ask determine our choices. What is free-will if we never truly exercise it?

It is the goal of higher consciousness to be able to free ourselves from the imprints and habit patterns that limit our free-will. The more we are able to exercise our free-will, the greater the possibility of achieving higher and higher consciousness and in a high-five to the virtuous circle, the higher the level of your consciousness, the greater capacity for free-will.

As we no longer think, feel, talk or act in an automatic and robotic manner, we become less and less predictable and therefore free from destiny. We become independent agents of change and the paths that we tread are no longer clear to the readers of the stars or any other indicators of destiny.

It is now clear that most of slumbering humanity is subject to the grinding wheels of destiny and have little influence over their successes or failures but there is always the pathless path of those who have chosen to exercise their free-will to de-program themselves and achieve freedom for themselves and become beacons of light for their brothers and sisters. May you decide to wake up from destiny's sleep and see the light of free-will.

# Grasp The Human Potential

One of the obstacles that beset all sincere spiritual aspirants is the doubt that arises from contemplating the amazing transformation of an essentially ignorant normal human being into an enlightened Master in one life-time. How is such a miracle even possible?

The great Masters have always taught that a human birth is a great opportunity for spiritual advancement. It is no wonder that we do not take their words as seriously as we should. This is because we are all too aware of human frailties and our disposition for negative actions, words and thoughts. However, the Masters keep teaching that even the gods are envious of a human birth. It is because we do not believe them in our hearts that we limit our spiritual progress.

We must take to heart that just as a seed cannot contemplate that one day it will grow to become a huge tree, just so a human being has all the potential to become an enlightened Master. The body-mind-soul complex of a normal human being can under the right circumstances unfold and develop into a cosmic being without limitations, just as with proper tending, sunlight and water, a seed can develop into an oak tree.

In spiritual yoga, we learn to develop the untapped potential of the life-force body with its energy centers (chakras) and energy channels (nadis) through the practice of pranayama and meditation. The sadhana or spiritual practice is the sunlight and water which transform the seed of spirituality within each human being.

A source of untapped power within us is that of Kundalini. Somehow, by a miracle of universal consciousness, this cosmic power lies dormant within every human being, waiting to be awakened whether in a million years or within this lifetime – it is our choice.

Just as the development of a seed takes its natural course and cannot normally be forced upon it, just so the unfolding of the cosmic being occurs in its natural rhythm per the efficiency of the practice. The spiritual practitioner should persevere and not be concerned about the rate of progress or time-frame for success because these are the result of doubt. The anxiety and stress from this doubt will delay the transformation as they infect the practice itself.

Each and every day, before beginning our practice, we should give thanks to the universal consciousness for our human birth and the potential invested in us. Let us put aside our doubts and set our sights firmly on the development of that potential with the unswerving dedication to the Masters who have and are still leading us from darkness to light.

# Don't Abuse Positive Thinking

There continues to be a proliferation of workshops, seminars, audios and books on the power of positive thought and the techniques of positive affirmations. These can be very misleading especially for those who have these "secrets" as their initial exposure to spirituality. I utilize affirmations in some of my workshops and so they certainly have a place on the spiritual path but they also have severe practical limitations that must be recognized.

Those who espouse the miracle of positive thinking point to the many testimonial successes that abound in print and in cyberspace. It is true that there is a certain percentage of those taking these workshops who initially report significant changes in their well-being and life-styles. However, when reality sets in, these initial successes are followed by disillusionment and even failure. There are basic psychological barriers that are deep in everyone's psyche that blocks the effectiveness of even the best examples of positive thinking and powerful affirmations.

The first factor is doubt and skepticism. No matter how much one tries to foster a set of positive beliefs, there is a part of our minds that will focus on the first sign that the power of positive thinking may not be working. Since it is not possible for everything to work out exactly perfectly due to external factors, the doubting mind has plenty of fuel to undermine the effects of positive thinking. Once it has 'proof' that it does not work, it will keep at it until one's confidence is gradually undermined over time – this is an inevitable vicious cycle because once undermined, the positive beliefs system becomes less and less effective and so more and more examples of its failure fuels the doubting mind.

The second mental factor that will reduce the effectiveness of any positive belief system is the negative self-esteem. This is the part of our mind that keeps whispering to us that we are not worthy for whatever the power of the new belief system promises. This is the voice that warns that things are going to go wrong, that we are not doing something right, or that everyone hates us etc. Even when something positive happens, it will whisper that it's not going to last! This negative voice is very difficult to silence once it gets going.

The above two factors keep our consciousness at a lower level and prevent us from achieving the promised potential of our humanity. That is the reason that Masters have given more powerful tools to overcome these barriers and many others that are obstacles to realization of our true Being. However, those tools require more effort and discipline and a regular practice to manifest their effectiveness – therefore, the need for a spiritual path such as yoga.

It is important to realize the difference between merely trying to foster a mental belief system through the power of positive thinking and a spiritual practice that eliminates the negative mental factors

that hold us back from our true potential.

# Is Karma Cruel?

Oftentimes, spiritual students are confused by their emotional nature and unable to come to terms with their intellectual understanding of the deeper aspects of life. It is then necessary to contemplate continuously on a truth in order to remove the emotional blockage. A mere reading or nodding acceptance is insufficient.

A few weeks ago, during a workshop for self-healing, I'd just finished explaining the purpose and mechanics of the law of Karma in order to instill in the listeners the discipline of taking personal responsibility for our current situation. This is particularly relevant in that the model I use places the ultimate cause for all health problems on the shoulders of our own karma – that is, we are responsible for our own health or lack thereof. It also means that we are responsible for our own healing and others are only able to help us along.

A question/comment from one of the students resonated with the rest of the audience – why does the law of Karma cause cancer and other deadly diseases to occur? Can't it function without 'causing so much suffering'?

From an emotional perspective, I would sympathize with these feelings. However, upon deeper reflection, one should be able to understand that the responsible party causing the suffering is not the law of Karma but the person who has triggered the law. Now, this is not a viewpoint that is popular to share because it is can indicate callousness towards those suffering. This is not true. We are all enmeshed in this cycle of karmic suffering – we are all in the same boat and recognizing how we all got there doesn't reduce our compassion for our fellow sufferers.

When a child touches the fire and burns her hand, we cannot blame the fire – it is its nature to burn. Even though we understand that it is the child's action that has caused the hurt, we do not cease to comfort the child or help in her healing. Her hurt is the consequence of her action and we do not ascribe human emotions such as cruelty to the fire.

Take a step further and suppose a drunken driver misses a warning road-sign and does not slow down around a curve – he crashes of the cliff. Can we blame the road-sign that is a warning? Can we blame the law of Gravity that caused the car and driver to plunge off the cliff? We know enough not to do so.

We can begin to understand that the law of Karma is based on the law of causation and is as impersonal as the law of Gravity. We cannot blame gravity for our weight or our inability to jump one hundred feet on earth. However, since we are indicating very personal events to karmic influences and it appears so complex because of the difficulty of identifying the appropriate causal chains to a particular effect, we may wish that the karmic law should take a more gentle approach. And indeed, most often it does. Unfortunately, gentle reminders get ignored and stronger measures become appropriate – it is like the warning signs on the road … first it is a road-sign, then comes road-bumps and then a road-block. There is an escalation in the karmic effects.

When we consider if the law of Karma can be more benign, we are forgetting that it has evolved over billions of years in how it operates on different beings in different realms. I personally consider the miracle of human childbirth to be a needlessly painful process for the mother.  However, nature has evolved this method as the most efficient one for mammals over hundreds of millions of years. We cannot ascribe cruelty to evolution.

Let us not project our emotional reactions onto a universal law such as Karma. We should broadly try to understand its nature and meditate to remove our anthropomorphic projections. Instead, we should heed the injunctions of the sages and modify our behavior to confirm to our higher nature and control our lower animal nature so that we can further evolve our consciousness.

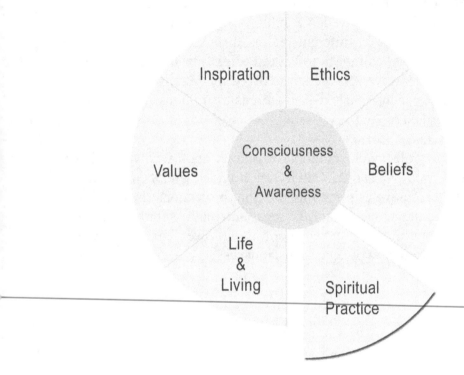

**Figure 7**
***Spiritual Practice***
***The Intentional Life Model***

# Spiritual Despair

Spiritual practitioners will sooner or later have to face a dramatic situation that has been highlighted by the opening chapter of the Bhagavadgita – the unwillingness to go forward to destroy our ignorance and negativities. This is not a platitude and is a tremendous test for the sincere seeker on the path and occurs only after considerable amount of prior effort.

To recap the scene, the hero Arjuna after 13 years of trials and tribulations has been guided by the Divine Lord Krishna to a great battle against the forces of darkness. Unfortunately, these forces of darkness arrayed before the hero happen to be his own kinsmen, some of whom he has great love and affection for. At this critical juncture, Arjuna decides that he would rather not fight and have to kill this own kith and kin. He throws down his weapons in despair.

This can be interpreted as a spiritual allegory – Arjuna is the sincere spiritual seeker who has been guided along the path by his teacher for many years. All his effort has been to annihilate the dark forces within his psyche. He had tried to live with them. He had tried to appease them by giving in to their demands constantly, but to not avail. They want to take over totally and will not even allow the seeker a sliver of light, love and joy. Finally, the seeker is led by his inner teacher to declare war and fight the inner darkness of desire, fear, pride and so on. However, when he confronts them he loses his motivation because they are also part of him and he has lived with them all his life – does he really want to rid himself of them? What will be become without them? Is it worth this personality surgery?

In fact, this is the stage when the practitioner finally has to face the reality that he or she has to destroy his ego and personality!

Most spiritual seekers do not really think very hard on what it means to achieve Self-Realization. It is only a theoretical consideration, if even that, when once in a while we are reminded that it is our ego, sensory mind and the personality that we've developed throughout our life that is the enemy standing between us and our True Self. We operate in the fuzzy view that everything will be fine and that we can just become better, stronger and more aware – that the ego will become subservient and our personality will become better because the negative aspects will disappear and we will have the ideal personality. Unfortunately, such a rosy picture does not reflect the reality of our karmic nature – the ego, sensory mind, and personality will not go away quietly.

When one realizes that state and faces that battle in earnest, it is almost universal that the seeker withdraws into despondency and even despair. In many cases, this happens even without the seeker being conscious of the reasons for these feelings – it happens to the practitioner who has been on the path for some years. This is a state of spiritual despair and should not be confused with lesser emotional problems or clinical depression. It can last for weeks or even years depending on the awareness of the seeker and the guidance of the teacher. In the case of Arjuna, it only lasted an hour or so because of the intervention of Lord Krishna, but this is exceptional.

There is another example set forth in famous Yoga Vashishtha – in that case, it was Lord Rama himself, a divine incarnation who in his youth become despondent and required the intervention of this family teacher, the Rishi Vashishtha to provide the guidance to overcome the lack of interest in human activity. This illustrates another spiritual barrier that advanced souls will face.

We can also find spiritual despair in the gospel of Lord Jesus when in the Garden of Gethsemane, he was temporarily overcome with despair which he resolved by power of will and surrender to his Father in heaven. It was the spiritual barrier of self-sacrifice.

It is probably not necessary for us to consider the state of a Lord Rama or Lord Jesus at this time, but we should keep in mind the experience of Arjuna who represents the sincere soul embarked on the path. Keep this in mind also when you or a friend on the path falls into spiritual despair.

The symptoms can be as mild as a lack of motivation and decrease in practice time or as severe as a total departure from the path. It is necessary to have a competent guide to help get back on the field of battle.

# Mindfulness

The mind in yoga is called manas and is our first level for experiencing the world through the senses. Manas is the sensory computer operating on the inputs from sight, hearing, smell, taste and touch. The ancients considered the mind to be a defining attribute for human beings – the first human is called Manu and humankind is called manava or the descendents of Manu.

In the Bhagavadgita, Lord Krishna has said that the mind can be one's best friend or one's worst enemy. If one has no control over one's own mind, then there can be no worst enemy who will defeat every positive effort. However, if one has control over one's mind, then it becomes a powerful ally to achieve one's goals. Therefore, control of the mind is essential to one's well-being as well as to the achievement of spiritual goals.

People suffer from stress and tension caused by worry and anxiety which in turn are caused by an overactive and uncontrolled mind. People suffer from unhappiness due to fears and desires which are caused by an uncontrolled mind. If a person can control his mind, then he will be free from suffering.

There are many methods of controlling the mind – in fact all meditation techniques are either focused on mind control or require a degree of control over mind.

Since the mind is distracted by external phenomena, the first stage would be to withdraw from external stimuli – which is why most meditation is done with the eyes closed and with mental attention drawn inward, focused on either a mental image, the breath or a part of the body.

The next stage to mind control is to develop concentration – this is where most of the effort is directed, as the mind tends to wander and is not focused on one point. Many years of effort may be needed in order to train the mind to be one-pointed. It is a tiring and difficult practice, but once achieved will open up a whole new world of experiencing that was previously denied due to all the noise of dispersion.

The third stage is achieved when concentration becomes effortless – this occurs when the mind and the object of meditation comes closer together and when there is an interchange of between object and subject and the subject partakes of some part of the object and gains insight into it. This is properly called the stage of meditation.

When the meditation deepens further, the mind and the object become so absorbed that they become one – this is the unity consciousness.

Through these stages, the mind becomes controlled. However, along the way, many distractions occur. Even when the mind is withdrawn from the external world in stage one, the mind becomes distracted by sub-conscious thoughts and memories and tend to pull the subject from the object, which is the reason for the difficulty in achieving a high degree of concentration. Perseverance is necessary.

Mindfulness is a state of awareness that is possible when one has achieved a high degree of concentration – it is practiced with the eyes open and the person interacting with the world. It would be very frustrating to try to practice this without first developing control of the mind. It is mindfulness which destroys all ego-centric behavior and lead to a harmonious and divine life free from sub-conscious compulsions.

# Overcoming Karmic Blocks

Just as Lord Shiva is the cosmic consciousness that guides us towards liberation from the cycle of birth and death through the practice of yoga, the power of Durga-ma can help to unlock the karmic hurdles that prevent us from living life in pursuit of liberation.

The stories about Durga-ma are always concerning her invocation by other gods to save them from some terrible demonic power. These stories have both a macrocosmic and microcosmic perspective.

The most famous story concerns the demon king Mahisaasur. He was so powerful that even though lacking any virtue, he was able to conquer the three worlds of humanity, demi-gods and gods. The gods rushed to the Divine Trinity for help and when the three Lords heard their sorry tale, they reacted with righteous anger and each emitted golden light which conjoined to give form to a young and lovely damsel. This was mother Durga with ten arms who was richly dressed in red and golden clothing and rode a fierce and fearless lion. She laughed and the world shook. She had the weapons bestowed by the other divine aspects – the trident from Lord Shiva, discus from Lord Vishnu, conch-shell from Varuna, flaming dart from Agni, the bow from Agni, the quiver and arrows from Surya, the iron rod from Yama, thunderbolt from Indra, the club from Kubera, the garland of snakes from Shesha and so on.

Durga-ma went on to defeat and kill Mahisaasur, of course. From a yogic perspective the demon lord personifies primordial ignorance and the might of the ego. When the spiritual student's positive characteristics as personified by the gods are separate and not unified, then she will suffer from the negative power of the ego. It is necessary to unify all of one's virtues in order to defeat ignorance and ego – this unification of all one's positive characteristics is called Durga-ma.

She is also called Chamunda for slaying Chanda and Munda who are the personifications of anger and passion. When these two demons hurled all their thousands of weapons at the Mother, she merely opened her mouth and absorbed them into her infinity without any harm.

Another strong demon called Raktabija had the power bestowed on him that every drop of his blood that touched the ground will give immediate birth to a clone of himself. He was the seed of desires and could not be killed – in fact, he multiplied himself as soon as he was cut down, just as the satisfaction of a desire gives rise to more desires. To overcome Raktabija, The Divine Mother stuck her lovely red tongue out and drank all the blood and consumed it – she is called mother Kali who can help us overcome our desires.

No matter what form she takes, she will help her devotees and punish the evil-doers. Since she is the mother of existence, she is also the giver of illusions as well as the remover of illusions. She will give the toys for her children to play if that is what they desire, or she will help them achieve to Self-Realization if that is what they aspire to.

Durge smrtaa harasi bhitima sheshajantoh
Svasthaih smrtaa matimativa shubhaam dadaasi
Daaridrya dukha bhayahaarini kaa tvadanaya
Sarvopakaara karanaaya sadaardracittaa.

O Mother Durga who relieves all difficulties, my fears are dispelled when I remember you
You increase the welfare and intelligence of the spiritual seekers who remember you

You are unique as you dispel poverty, pain and fear and extend
compassion to all
We bow to you who reveal the Divine Consciousness to those who
meditate.

# The Importance of Sacrifice in Yoga

Sacrifice or Yagna is a pivotal concept in the Sanatana Dharma. It is
one that is not really explored much in popular treatments of yogic
philosophy. However, sacrifice permeates all levels of spirituality.

In one of the creation myths, it is the sacrifice of the first being,
Prajapati that gives rise to the rest of creation! In another myth, it is
the sacrifice of Sati, the first wife of Lord Shiva which made possible
the 51 shakti-piths or centers of the Divine Mother for the welfare of
humanity – each of the piths has the essence of one part of her body.

In the ancient Vedas, sacrifice is the primary means of attaining to
the higher realms and or achieving success in this world. The priests
would perform the sacrifice on behalf of the sponsor, who would
usually be a king and like a correctly performed science experiment,
the results desired would be fulfilled by compelling the responsible
deity to discharge his duties.

In the Bhagavad-gita, we find that instead of an externally performed
sacrifice by someone else, the emphasis is now on either an internal
sacrifice or at the least action performed by oneself.

The definition of sacrifice now becomes selfless action, that is, any
actions performed without regard to one's own welfare but for the

sake of others would be yagna. Thus the fire of yagna is fueled either by a sense of duty or compassion. Whatever one's circumstances, one has assumed certain duties whether voluntarily or by birth, and the selfless commission of one's duties is as a sacrifice. If one does not have a specific duty towards another, but still chooses to act out of compassion, it is also a yagna.

The sacrificial act is self-less and consequently without karmic impact – this is very important, since if one completes a kind action for another, one would acquire good karma, but just as bad karma should be avoided, even good karma will bind us in the cycle of birth and death. It is only non-karmic acts that don't bind us, and therefore sacrifice is the essence of Karma Yoga.

The performance of sacrifice is connected with dispassion and non-attachment because only with non-attachment to the results of one's actions can the yagna be perfect.

All spiritual practices which lead towards Self-Realization are also considered to be sacrifice. This is because the sadhana is not done with any material benefit in mind and to be able to achieve Self-Realization, there has to be a dispassion towards the results as well.

Therefore, the process of Yoga is an internal sacrifice which results in the state of Yoga or union with one's true Self. It is the attainment of divine knowledge and wisdom which liberates one form the cycle of birth and death.
It is stated in the Bhagavad-gita:

> Apaane juhvati praanam praane'paanam tathaapare
> Praanaapaana gati ruddhvaa praanaayaama paraayanaah

Those who practice yoga as a sacrifice by offering the inhaled breath into the exhaled breath and the exhaled breath into the inhaled breath, achieve the breathless super-conscious state.

It is this verse that emphasizes to all those who practice Kriya Yoga that their practice is the internal fire ceremony or sacrifice and it is the death of desires burned in the fire of breath that leads to the immortal spirit.

# Beware Spiritual Materialism

*Meditation leads to fleeting peace*
*Drugs lead to fleeting euphoria*
*Do not trust in fleeting states of mind*

*Attachment to impermanent states*
*Leads to increase of ego I-ness*
*Trust not in temporal states of mind*

*Cessation of passing peace and joy*
*Suffering destroys each mental toy*
*Do not trust in fleeting states of mind*

*Ever vigilant, strive for refuge divine*
*Ever constant, practice death of ego I-ness*
*Trust not in in temporal states of mind.*

# Overcome The Effect Of Vritti

Human suffering is due to our identification with the vritti or fluctuations of the mind. Vritti can take the form of thoughts, feelings, emotions and abstract concepts. It is the vritti which binds us to an object – when one identifies with the vritti and through the vritti with the object. Suffering arises when one identifies with the vritti of his or her physical body and consequently with the physical body itself – "I am this body!" When someone else's body is diseased, one does not feel the pain but when one's own body is sick, the one thinks that "I am sick," due to the ego identifying with that body.

One method of overcoming this effect of vritti is by the method of Silent Witnessing (Sakshi Bhava). There are two modes of practice:

1.      Dedicated practice – sit as in meditation with back straight and body relaxed, watch your thoughts, feelings and emotions without identifying with them. Do not try to stop them but try not to react to them either. It is as if you've split yourself into two selves – one that is having the vritti and the other one is the silent witness who only watches with awareness.

2.      Daily activity practice – this is a more advanced technique when one becomes the silent witness during all of one's activities such as driving, walking, talking, working, bathing, brushing teeth, eating etc. It will be easier if one practices initially for a short time such as during solitary meals or morning toiletries rather than during talking or interaction with others. As you become more proficient, then you can include more complex tasks.

It is said that Yogananda encouraged his disciples to go to the theatre and watch movies so that they could experience the world as merely another projection of the divine mind. However, we often get emotionally involved with the characters or activities in a movie and start identifying with them. Success in Sakshi Bhava requires identifying with the spirit or atman and not the body or mind – this overcomes the ego's identification with this body vritti generated by the mind. During the practice, you become the Sakshi or silent witness and watch your other self as if appearing in a movie. This practice first loosens the grip of the ego, lessens the suffering of mis-identification and increases peace and contentment.

# What Meditation Is Not

Meditation is absorption in a chosen object or subject. It happens when the practitioner develops a high state of concentration. Basically, concentration requires effort to stay in that state while no effort is required in meditation. The important point is that meditation cannot occur without exceptional concentration which in turn requires higher mental development and the ability to withdraw from the distraction of the five senses. Meditation can occur only when the mind is controlled. Those with an uncontrolled mind cannot meditate – they are in the practice phase of controlling the mind.

There are other mental functions and practices which are often confused by the uninitiated seeker as meditation. It will be helpful to remove such confusions from our minds in order for us to make progress to reach the state of meditation. As always, the word in spiritual context refers to both the path and state of consciousness.

The process of thinking is not meditation. Whether it is the usual stream of thoughts or a directed problem solving mode of thought, the effort required, the energy expanded, the fatigue that sets in and the confusion that normally results differentiate this mental mode from meditation. Only when a person has achieved a high state of concentration that problem solving becomes fully directed and not meandering.

Another mental mode that we slip into easily is day-dreaming where we try to escape from the pressures and conflicts in our lives and reproduce some comforting or enjoyable alternate reality. This fantasy mode of thought enmeshes us more in our own confusion and does not provide the mental clarity that is a mark of meditation. During the process of day-dreaming, we sometimes momentarily lose awareness of our consciousness or space-out. This has no benefit and is not a mark of higher consciousness or the state of meditation, but only a relapse into the unconscious state.

The practice of repeating affirmations can be helpful in overcoming some superficial or simple mental blocks. When this is supplemented with the relaxation techniques from self-hypnosis, deeper mental problems can be tackled. However helpful these are, neither can provide the insights of meditation.

Another practice that is helpful is the use of prayers in trying to focus our needs and intentions. We invoke a higher order of being to help us in prayers. Praying is a spiritual practice but is not meditation. Praying should not be confused with the use of mantras or Sanskrit power sounds. Certain mantras can be used in the path of Mantra Yoga to achieve a concentrated and absorbed mind leading to meditation.

Finally, the use of mind altering drugs is not meditation. Such substances can stimulate different states of consciousness but they are hardly under any kind of control as the subconscious may be given free reign of the mind. There is some confusion as drugs are used sometimes as the main focus of a spiritual path or as a supplement to certain techniques, but in all cases, they are substitutes to meditation.

It is unwise to use the word meditation without a precise understanding of what it means and what it doesn't mean. This will prevent us from falling into mental traps that will delay our spiritual progress.

# Your Hands Can Affect Your Meditation

What are your hands doing when you are trying to meditate? When a seeker enters the stream and take a path of spiritual insight, he or she will pay a lot of attention to the sitting position and body posture. However, not much attention is paid initially to the position of the hands and this oversight can be detrimental to progress in meditation.

Traditionally, different hand positions have been established to have different effects on the energetic, emotional and mental processes. This is called the science of mudras and can be observed in statues and paintings of divinities and masters of yoga.

From a meditation perspective, the right combination of hand positions can either hinder or help depending on the type of meditation. There needs to be a matching – no single mudra is the best for all types of meditation techniques or situations.

For mindfulness or contemplative techniques which require sitting still for long periods, closed energy mudras may be best, so as to reduce the loss of energy. Simple mudras such as clasping the fingers of the hands together or with one hand resting on the other at the level of the naval are great energy savers. A third mudra for quiet meditation is the crossed arms or svastika mudra with the hands resting on the inside of the elbows.

For mantra meditation where a rosary or mala is used, you might want to have your left hand with the palms up at the naval level, while the right hand is holding the rosary at the heart level. The lower part of the rosary can be resting on the left palm.

In the case of energetic meditations where prana (life-force energy) or kundalini shakti (evolutionary energy) is being raised or expanded, additional help in controlling the mind is required. This is because a turbulent or distracted mind will affect the movement of the energy and cause unintended consequences. To prevent mental disturbances, both hands can be placed in chin mudra, where the tip of each index finger is touching the tip of the thumb to form a small circle. This brings about an energetic connection that helps to control the movements of the mind. A variation is to have one hand in chin mudra and the other in jnana mudra with the index finger touching the inside of the crease of the thumb below the tip. The jnana mudra helps to stimulate the wisdom potential of the mind.

A final note for those who are fortunate to have the opportunity to practice in the company of a master yogi – you should present an open hand posture to better receive the energy and blessings of the master. It is recommended to put your hands on the knees with the palms facing outwards or upwards.

Whatever practice or tradition a student is engaged in, proper attention should be applied to the placement of the hands for maximum benefit.

# Five Verses On Spiritual Practice

The great spiritual reformer and teacher, Shankaracharya wrote voluminous commentaries and treatises but when asked to give the core essence for spiritual seekers, he composed five verses called the "The Essence of Spiritual Practice in Five verses." Let us look at the first two verses:

*Study the scriptures diligently*
*Perform well the rituals and actions as described in the scriptures*
*Worship god through the performance of ritual*
*Keep the mind from desire-originated actions*

*Let your sins be destroyed*
*Let the seeker inquire into the defects of re-incarnation*
*Make a firm resolve to attain to the True Self*
*Leave your own home immediately*
*Verse 1*

The first verse is the preparatory phase – the phase of the worldly person engaged in activity who is making an effort to learn more about spirituality. One should refer to reliable and time-tested works of wisdom to engage in the study of the self –this should be done regularly in order to overcome the resistance of our materialistic tendencies. In the days of the Shankaracharya, it was customary for each person to perform his or her own rituals of worship, rather than go to a priest and every youth was taught the proper methods and mantras for this purpose. We are advised not to utilize the rituals for the sake of material gain or for pleasure but for the sake of removal our negativities so that we can move forward towards liberation from karma. A meditation that the acharya recommends is to recollect the pain and suffering involved with re-birth driven by the wheel of karma. Once sufficient positive tendencies and good habits have been cultivated and a distaste for cycle of birth and death, then one is ready to make the resolution to seek Self-Realization. The advice to leave one's home should be understood from the perspective of the time when it was necessary to journey great distances to find a Master who could guide the seeker towards the final goal and also the need for staying at an ashram for extended periods of time in order to gain the wisdom necessary. At the present time, it may not be necessary to go to such an extreme as with the communication age, everything seems to be within reach – spiritual teachers travel all over the world and there are workshops and retreats galore. However, it is good to keep in mind the level of dedication that the acharya is advocating and examine our own use of time and resources. Certainly, a re-alignment even for the house-holder is necessary as a serious spiritual practice requires a minimum of several hours per day!

*Seek the company of the wise in satsang*
*Develop firm devotion to Brahman*

*[139]*

*Develop virtuous qualities mental tranquility and restraint of*
*senses*
*Let him renounce all rituals*
*Let him approach a wise sage*
*Let him serve the sage*
*Then let him inquire about the indestructible Brahman*
*Let him hear the mahavakyas – the essence of the Vedas*
*Verse 2*

Once we have started on the spiritual journey in earnest, then one should cultivate the company of the spiritual Masters and try to listen to them whenever possible – even watching videos or listening to CDs are acceptable. One should now drop all rituals or worship and focus on devotion to the one Divine with meditation on the vastness and orderliness of the universe and by singing praises of the Eternal Now. The acharya recommends simultaneously the cultivation of virtues such as non-violence, truthfulness, non-stealing etc., in order to qualify for becoming a spiritual disciple. It is necessary to make a search for a sage – one who has attained to the state of Self-Realization – the search should include common-sense research to ensure one is not taken in by someone who is either deluded or making a pretence of their level of perfection. Once one has decided on the Master and prepared one-self appropriately, one can then approach such a Master with humility and an attitude of service. In olden days, the seeker would be required to stay at the ashram from one to three years taking care of the place and looking after the needs of the Master, during which time, he will be tested time and again to ensure that he is ready for the higher teachings. Nowadays, the service would be more fund-raising or organization-oriented and will be defined by the Master. When the Master indicates that the seeker is ready, then the seeker becomes a disciple and will be given the appropriate guidance and direction whether by the imparting of wisdom or the bestowal of a spiritual practice depending on the type of path that is chosen.

Let's examine the third verse:

*Now, reflect on the essence of the mahavakyas from the Upanishads*
*only*
*Stop all unnecessary discussions or speculations and focus only on*
*revealed wisdom*
*Remain absorbed in the attitude of "I am Brahman"*
*Renounce feelings of pride and arrogance*
*Give up the identification with the body*
*Give up argumentation with the sages*

The second verse ended with the spiritual aspirant established as the student of a sage and learning at the feet of his Master. When he has learned all that can be learned from the teachings of his preceptor, then it is time for the student to reflect on what has been transmitted. This would typically be the great sayings of the philosophical treatises called the Upanishads which have been sanctioned by generations of sages and shown to lead to the experience of the divine union with one's true Self. The great sayings are called mahavakyas – an example is "Aham Brahmasmi" or "God and I, me and God, are one."

There is a tendency for the student to get side-tracked into other philosophical debates or speculations which are not central to his realization and this must be avoided in order not to waste time and resources. One should remain steadfast in one's contemplation.

All the mahavakyas and indeed all the Upanishads are meant to lead to the realization that the soul is spirit and spirit and God are one. In order to achieve this realization, it is necessary to make an adjustment in our attitudes towards one another and towards the world – we cannot act in a manner inconsistent with this teaching and so we cannot act selfishly or in an ordinary manner but would have to "love one's neighbor as one-Self."

When one has an attitude of being united with the divine, there is a tendency to be touched by pride and arrogance, however subtly and this has to be avoided and consciously renounced.

The cause of suffering is our disunity from our true nature and subsequent identification with the body. This physical nature is all that we can know with our five senses and so we have grown to think that it is all there is to reality and therefore we must be our physical body. Together with the right attitude of identifying with the divine is the giving up of the wrong attitude of thinking we are the body.

Once we are established in the right attitude and renounced erroneous ones, we begin to achieve the actual experience of the unity that we have previously only intellectually understood. As we start to glimpse reality, there is a tendency to start sharing with others the truths that we are now convinced that we know. This can lead to confusion and subtle errors because only when we are fully established in wisdom do we realize that reality cannot be discussed or argued upon as it is beyond our normal consciousness and language. Reality is neither dual or non-dual or combination of both. In higher consciousness, we can experience reality as it is but when we come down to the relative world, where something either exists or not exists, all concepts fail to adequately describe it and so there can be no end to dispute. The normal mind is not equipped to deal with reality, only with a four dimensional space-time splice of reality. Shankaracharya therefore counsels that against arguing with sages.

In the first verse, the acharya counseled the seeker on achieving a steady resolve towards the spiritual path, followed in the second verse with seeking the sage to hear his wisdom. In the third verse, the student needs to reflect on what has been transmitted and acquire his own discriminative awareness.

In the fourth verse, the great teacher examines how the spiritual practitioner should live the material life.

*Practice moderation in food*
*Fasting can heal diseases*
*Live contentedly upon whatever comes to you as a blessing from*
*the divine*

*Endure all the pairs of opposites: heat and cold, and the like.*
*Avoid wasteful talks.*
*Practice equanimity*
*Desire not the kindness of others*

Obviously, one must support oneself or one's family in a suitable manner but should not run after excessive requirements, living in contentment with what has been allotted by the universal grace. Practicing moderation in food and fasting at least one day every week builds self-control as well as keeps the practitioner in good health. It is easy to become concerned about one's comfort which can lead to igniting desires for what is liked and aversion to what is not liked. It is important to seek balance in life which can be upset by keeping company with those who are seeking material goals. If the practitioner seeks help from others, it puts her in debt to those who offer support and this must be repaid sooner or later, enmeshing her in the material cycle of action and reaction. Of course, if someone offers unsolicited help, it is not necessary to reject it. In all activities, the practitioner's goal is to stay calm and centered.

In the fifth and last verse, the practitioner's spiritual progress is examined.

*In solitude live joyously.*
*Quieten your mind in the Supreme Lord.*
*Realize and see the All-pervading Self everywhere.*
*Recognize that the finite Universe is a projection of the Self.*
*Conquer the effects of the deeds done in earlier lives by the present right action.*
*Through wisdom become detached from future actions.*

The sage is now united and abides in his true Self, ever in bliss irrespective of the circumstances, and being ever mindful of the Divine. This is an internal state of super-consciousness which is attained during deep Samadhi meditation. The next step is to extend the internal realization to dealing with the apparently external world which is accomplished through first seeing that one's true Self pervades everything and the apparent diversity is united in the Self – we are all One. In the next stage, the whole of the universe is seen as only a manifestation of the Self and without a separate existence. In this divine consciousness state, all past karma is wiped clean as if it never existed and the sage now acts only in the present without ego or karma.

# Nothing Seems To Happen?

Too often I hear from sincere seekers that they are trying their best and putting in persistent effort but nothing seems to be happening with their meditation. It gets very boring and they are tempted to give up. Doubts arise that maybe the meditation is not right for them or maybe they are not right for the meditation. What's up with this? Shouldn't there be a way to know what's happening with one's meditation?

It is critical to remember that no matter what form of meditation we are doing, the goal is to remove the obstacles that have accumulated in our mental, emotional, energetic and physical bodies that prevent us from experiencing our true blissful nature. In the physical body, our nervous system has been wired from birth with stressful obstructions which need to be cleared away before we can regain our center. It is the same with our mental and emotional bodies. It is the reason that we seem to be overcome by mental and emotional blockages.

Remember that the practices of yoga are for cleansing the karmic blockages and so you know they are working when the thoughts and emotions arise during your meditation! These are the indications that something is being released. Unfortunately, we get hung up with what is being released and oftentimes, we try to fixate on that rather than maintaining our calm during this cleansing process. When you clean house, you don't keep the garbage that is the result, and so you should not keep back the thoughts and emotions which are released during the meditation – they need to be let go of.

We are so used to projecting our minds outward that when we try to focus inward, we get confused and don't understand what is going on. Instead of practicing, we start thinking about what we should be experiencing. One must understand that the mind is continuously in motion. When one is awake, the mind acts as a sensory computer monitoring the five inputs of sight, sound, taste, smell and touch and when one is asleep, the mind takes the memories and re-organizes them to provide dreams. Only when one reaches the state of dreamless sleep does one get a rest from the mind. In the same way, only after the cleansing of karmic blockages is achieved does the mind become restful and the soul can experience its natural Spirit nature.

Accept what is happening during meditation and try not to judge or expect something different – it is what it is – it is what is now. A lot is happening during your meditation. When one says that nothing is happening, it means that what is happening is not what we expect should be happening – this is a mental trap that keeps us from our happiness. When a lot of thoughts come, it is progress and when very little or no thoughts come, it is also progress.

Relax and let the process unfold. Persevere in your practice and eventually, you will experience the bliss of your true Self.

# Choose Your Yoga Cautiously

Most spiritual seekers are not aware that there can be significant differences between powerful yogic systems that can affect their ability to function in society.

The yogic systems that were developed and flourished during the last two thousand years were influenced by the advent of the dark age and required total dedication from their practitioners. Such systems are meant for a reclusive life-style. The successful practitioners were monks and celibates who dwelled in caves or monasteries, away from society. There were very few systems that were developed for the house-holder.

You might think that this historical background is not relevant to the spiritual seeker today, since yoga has been promulgated to the West and disseminated to a larger segment of the population than ever before. However, unfortunately, much of the yogic systems still have their roots in medieval India and have been mostly taught by monks or disciples of monks. There is nothing wrong with monks and I'm not trying to belittle their achievements in transmitting the yogic teachings through the dark ages – it is through their dedication that we still have the true yogic teachings. My only concern is that the techniques and systems are not meant for householders.

The powerful yogic techniques in some of these systems speed up our spiritual evolution through the rapid unfolding of our karma which can cause great physical, emotional and mental stress. The changes caused by the techniques are so dis-orienting that it is necessary to be under the supervision of a competent guide. The stress on the practitioner is such that he or she will not be able to carry on a career or even a relationship, not to mention taking care of a family. Unfortunately, there are no cautionary voices or even when there are, they are drowned out by the ubiquitous availability of all types of techniques and practices in books and on the internet.

One should never practice any technique without understanding its possible effects. Consider that before we take any prescription drug, we need to know about its possible side-effects, but apparently not for life-altering yogic techniques.

Find out about the roots of the yogic system, not just the current head or teacher. Research whether it was required to be a celibate or a monk in the past. Even if updated for this generation, find out if a Master was involved in the changes. Only a Master can make the changes necessary to keep a system effective and yet customize it for a new generation. Seek out other householder students or teachers of the system and get their experience.

Many spiritual students are bewildered when they practice diligently and find their lives falling apart. This is not because they are doing anything wrong. It is because they have chosen the yogic system that may not be meant for a householder practitioner.

# What is Kriya Yoga?

There are many different types of yoga systems and according to their proponents, each must be the best. This can be very confusing to sincere seekers but there may be no easy solution to differentiate these various paths in their minds. It is the nature of the mind to be confused due to karmic obstacles and desires which can lead one to ignore one solution and grasp for another. If the seeker strives to listen to the heart, then eventually the best path for this life-time will present itself. Until then, one should practice to one's best capacity whatever one has had the good fortune to learn.

It would not be prudent to present any one path as being the best or right one for all seekers since if that was true, then there would not be the necessity for so many different systems. However, it is possible to describe and compare different paths – this is a reasonable act in accordance with our discriminatory faculties.

Kriya Yoga is a system for Self-Realization that has been taught since time immemorial and so there is a lineage and a procession of realized Masters who have achieved their liberation through its practice. It is said to be the practical system that underlies the Yoga of Patanjali and from which he derived his descriptive sutras. There is a great deathless being called Mahavatar Babaji who has initiated many Masters such as Shankaracharya and even some Avatars (manifestations of divinity to help humanity) into Kriya Yoga.

In modern times, Babaji has once again graced us with this practice through his great disciple Yogiraj Shri Shri Shyamcharan Lahiri Mahasaya who received it on our behalf in 1861 in the Himalayan ranges. The present lineage of Masters included Swami Shri Yuteswara and Paramhansa Yogananda. The living Himalayan Master, Yogiraj Siddhanath is from this lineage. The lives and teachings of these Masters attest to the efficiency and effectiveness of Kriya Yoga.

One of the distinctive marks of Kriya Yoga is its power and simplicity to achieve Self-Realization. It utilizes both meditation on the primal sound of Om and spinal breathing techniques. According to Lahiri Mahasaya, "Aum and Kriya constitute the secret of meditation. By meditation on Aum and the practice of Kriya pranayama, the fulfillment of the highest spiritual aspiration is attained."

The spinal breathing meditation works on the spinal energy centers which evolve human consciousness to superhuman consciousness, speeding up our spiritual evolution. As Yogananda explains in his *Autobiography of a Yogi*, "The Kriya Yogi mentally directs his life energy to revolve, upward and downward, around the six spinal centers (medullary, cervical, dorsal, lumbar, sacral, and coccygeal plexuses) which correspond to the twelve astral signs of the zodiac, the symbolic Cosmic Man. One half-minute of revolution of energy around the sensitive spinal cord of man effects subtle progress in his evolution; that half-minute of Kriya equals one year of natural spiritual unfoldment."

Kriya Yoga is a scientific process to enable our evolving soul to gradually realize its fundamental unity with the immortal Spirit. Swami Satyananda, another disciple of Shri Yukteshwar is quoted as saying, "Kriya sadhana (spiritual practice) may be thought of as the sadhana of the practice of being in Atman (Spirit)"

The process of Kriya Yoga requires the raising of our dormant potentiality called Kundalini. A modern Master, Yogiraj Siddhanath has said, "By the ceaseless movement of the Kriya life-force breath, one's prana, breath, vital fluid and mind become one to form the evolutionary life-force energy called kundalini."

Kriya Yoga is a means of overcoming all our karmic obstacles to happiness and contentment. It is the path towards liberation from suffering, a goal that can be achieved within a single life-time if performed with dedication and perseverance. Unlike some other paths, it does not require its practitioners to leave their family, friends and vocation to stay in the hidden caves of the Himalayas. Kriya Yoga is meant for contemporary householders and to help them to be in the world but not of the world while pursuing life's greatest goal.

# Signs of Progress in Pranayama

A primary yogic practice is the use of breath to control the life-force energy and direct it to awaken our potential divinity. A spiritual path such Kriya Yoga is structured such that most of the practitioner's sadhana is based on the pranayama according to the principle that prana and mind are directly linked and mastering prana leads to mastery of mind and the awakening of higher consciousness. Kriya pranayama merges seamlessly into Dhyana and eventually Samadhi.

All sincere practitioners will experience certain signs during the course of their daily efforts and there always arise questions about whether these are positive or negative. I'm relating the main milestones that are common to everyone so that you can feel re-assured that there is no cause for concern. However, there may be other symptoms which are specific to certain physiologies and karmic dispositions and cannot be covered in a general article.

One of the first effects of pranayama is the occurrence of heat and sweat. This is caused by the purification that is taking place in the physical and subtle bodies and are good signs of progress. The perspiration carries the impurities out with it. Gradually, the perspiration will decrease as the bodies become more purified. If the sweat becomes a distraction, rub it into the body or if there is too much, use a towel to wipe it away before continuing the practice. Sometimes a side-effect of the purification is restlessness which can be addressed with improved posture and mental control.

The navel chakra or manipura is one of the first subtle energy centers to be affected by pranic practice. Sometimes air or gurgling sounds can be present in the digestive system. The primary positive sign is the feeling of heat or light in the navel as the fire element is transformed into a dynamic spiritual power called tejas. The purification of the digestive system is closely related to the transformation of the nervous and endocrine systems.

With the opening of the higher chakras, one starts to experience colored lights and various sounds. Sometimes some sadhaks get confused that the sounds are caused by a physical malady called tinnitus. These pranic sounds are such that when one does not focus internally, the sounds tend to disappear. During certain practices, the sounds can be quite overwhelming but in a positive way. One does not get irritated by them. There is no need to dwell too much on them either as they are like sign-posts on the road – one should keep practicing and not be diverted by thinking of them.

As your pranayama progresses, you may spontaneously enter into blissful states. These can be quite pleasant and there is always the questions whether to stop the practice and follow the bliss. It is generally better to continue the practice. The reason is that these blissful interludes are sporadic and may disappear in a month or a year as different karmic configurations come into play. The regular practice leads to Self-Realization and a continuous blissful state that is not dependent on karma.

I hope this helps to settle some of the questions in the minds of sincere practitioners. Due to the lack of personal guidance, many seekers get confused and stop practicing because they don't know if they are doing something wrong. Spiritual progress can get delayed because of doubts and irregular discipline. Seek out a qualified guide, follow u proven system and don't get diverted by doubts.

# The Moon In Kriya Yoga

As we learn of the passing of a true hero, that of Neil Armstrong who took a small step on the Moon and expanded the boundaries of humanity, I'm reminded of the significance of the moon as a powerful symbol in the yogic tradition. Just as the effect of Armstrong's feat will take generations to be felt, the effect of the moon principle is hidden although manifest in all our thoughts.

In Yoga, the moon is a symbol of the mind. The moon is fast moving and waxes and wanes, sometimes dark and hidden and sometimes bright and shinning. The mind is restless and fast moving - it is moody and changing, sometimes happy and sometimes sad. The moon can only be seen at night and is hidden in the day just as the mind is hidden in activity and only when one stops and reflects on it, does one begin to unravel its mysteries.

There is a dark side of the moon which is hidden from our view just as there is a portion of the mind that is hidden from us, that of the subconscious. The moon has no light of its own and can only reflect the light of the sun, just as the mind has no volition and direction without the light of the soul.

The moon in Hatha yoga is associated with the left energy channel called the ida nadi in the subtle body while the sun is associated with the right energy channel called the pingala nadi. The goal is to balance the sun and the moon in order to awaken the hidden potential called the Kundalini Shakti.

In Kriya Yoga, we are going beyond balancing and seek to actively merge the moon with the sun - that is to have the soul-spirit take control of the mind. In the first phase, the sun-fire is in the navel chakra or energy center and when it rises to the moon above the soft palate of the mouth, it causes the diffusion of the nectar of bliss which permeates the sensory mind to keep it under control. The moon-mind is like an unruly animal and must be tamed and controlled in order for the higher consciousness of wisdom-bliss to arise.

*[152]*

When the mind is somewhat controlled, it becomes possible for the moon-matter at the first chakra to merge with the sun-light at the third-eye center and this gives rise to a unity consciousness that transcends the moon-mind. In fact, the Kriya Yogi experiences the state of no-mind because she is now in the integrated super and supra-awareness state.

All this may seem a little esoteric to you but is nevertheless experientially verifiable during the course of sincere yogic practice.

Just as the moon is not the master of our solar system, so realize that the mind is not the master of our self and that there is the sun that gives the light and life to our external world just as there is the Self that bestows the light and life to our subjective world. If we want to really realize the truth, we can experience that even the material sun is enlightened by our subjective Self, which is merged into the Universal Consciousness.

A journey, no matter how short or long, begins with a first step and just as Armstrong has helped humanity on the journey to the stars by taking that first step on the moon, so also, the yogis of the past have taken the steps that will help humanity journey to the heights of our evolution.

# The Spiritual Eye in Kriya Yoga

A theme that was consistently emphasized in the teachings of Yogavatar Lahiri Mahasaya, the polestar of Kriya Yoga, is that of the spiritual eye. He called it the Kutastha Chaitanya. It is equivalent to the third-eye center or Ajna chakra which is located in the third ventricle of the brain in the middle of the head behind the mid-eye brow.

All the sages have said that the Divine is within us and that we can realize our unity with the Divine. Lahiri Mahasya has identified the spiritual eye as the center through which one can attain to this Divine consciousness, because "it is the center of two-fold consciousness where the individual self meets the Cosmic Self."

By the practice of Kriya breath and the Jyoti Mudra (an advanced technique of Kriya Yoga), the door to Divine Consciousness is revealed. It appears in the spiritual eye as a bright light – in the Master's words – "the Divine Light illumines the spiritual eye. Within that bright light is revealed a blue center. It is a vibrant and yet serene light of solid blue. Further, within this blue center shines a star, the guiding light."

It is the guiding light of this star revealed in the spiritual eye that fills the Kriya practitioner with a soothing peace that cannot be articulated and protects her from all desires throughout the hustle and bustle of daily life. It is the guiding light of this star that fills the Kriya adept with a self-less love that eventually stops the flow of the karmic wheel of life and death. It is the guiding light that fills the Kriya adept with the power of higher consciousness that eventually leads to the unity with the cosmic Divine Consciousness.

The Divine Light revealed in the spiritual eye shines in all the other lotus centers – the spiritual chakras along the central astral channel called sushumna nadi. It transforms all these pranic centers so that they each reveal their own levels of illumination in different spheres of consciousness to envelope the whole of existential Being.

Only when the whole self is realized can the soul-self merge with the Divine Self and attain Divine Consciousness. Lahiri Mahasya identifies this process as a second birth, "when the individual self-consciousness enters the cosmic Self-Consciousness, soul is reborn in God. This is the mystic second birth."

When one is truly re-born, one enters into Samadhi immersed in the Divine Light and experiences the infinite bliss of consciousness, the absolute universal peace and the timeless eternity of existence.

# Nectar Of Immortality

One of the most hidden treasures of yogic knowledge is that of Soma or Amrita – the nectar of immortality and bliss. There are lots of misinformation and confusion on this subject and unfortunately very little in the way of clarity because of the sacredness of the knowledge. It is sacred because of its profound effect and mysterious because it cannot be experienced without the proper consciousness.

In the ancient Vedic scriptures, it appears that Soma is the substance that is offered to the gods – however its description is couched in mystery and no clear information is given on how to manufacture that Soma. This has not stopped the experiments or claims that the extract from this moon plant or other will yield the fabled nectar. Disappointment seems to follow all such claims.

There are numerous passages where Soma is associated with the word suta (meaning pressed or squeezed) and there are verses which say that the god Indra became intoxicated after drinking the Soma and was able to destroy the cosmic serpent that was wrapped around the cosmic egg. However, in the Rig Veda 10.85.3, it is also said, "Those priests may regard Soma as a creeper which is crushed for getting its juice for use in the ritual. But to the seers, Soma is not something to be drunk." Therefore there seems to be multiple meanings for Soma even within the Vedas.

In the later mythical stories, a stronger hint is given for the manufacture of this nectar. There is the story of the churning of the great universal ocean of milk by means of the cosmic serpent wrapped around a sacred mountain – this imagery would now evoke the raising of the potential energy called Kundalini in the astral spine. We may then suspect that the nectar is something that is produced by the raising of this Kundalini energy, which is the result of certain yogic and tantric practices.

This becomes even clearer when we consult the early medieval text from the Mahayogi, Shiva-Goraksha-Babaji:

> *Who seal bindu by jewel of Kechari*
> *Even embraced by heavenly damsels*
> *Their essence does not fall to waste*
> *Instead they immortal soma taste*

The later yogic texts all subscribe to the identification of Soma as a substance secreted by the yogi's body as a result of perfecting certain practices and attaining a higher consciousness. The practice most often cited is that of Kechari Mudra which stimulate the production and retention of the nectar. It is not possible to go into detail to talk about this advanced technique although it is described in various texts because there are also lots of mistaken lore about it. My advice is to only practice this mudra after proper initiation and verbal instruction.

It is necessary to understand that the texts all say that the nectar can only be attained through the Kechari mudra. However, the majority only focus on the physical attainment of lengthening their tongues but neglect to practice the stilling of the mind. The Kechari stops the movement of prana or life-force energy in the side channels and enables it to move into the central channel. When the prana moves properly in the central channel, the mind stills and the practitioner enters into a heightened state of awareness. Even then, the nectar is not produced unless the Kundalini rises in the central channel and that can only happen if there is sufficient sexual essence or prana to fuel its passage. A period of celibacy is required for such an endeavor.

You might now be rather bemused by the technicalities involved and that is good because it is my goal only to caution against the premature practice of this Kechari mudra for the sake of tasting the Soma. I will also caution against trying to find this nectar through experimenting with drugs or plants – that is also doomed to failure and can also lead to negative karmic effects.

So, what am I trying say? Persevere in your spiritual practice and the Soma will be secreted when the right conditions are present. It is a by-product of higher consciousness and not something to be desired after for its own sake.

# The Glory of the Unstruck Sound

When a spiritual practitioner's subtle body becomes purified and there is a withdrawal of the senses from the external environment towards the internal center, she will experience various inner sounds. These should not be confused with the physical sounds of the body resulting from the rushing of blood or contraction of various organs. These inner sounds can lead to higher consciousness.

Many seekers have mistakenly been bothered by hearing a persistent "noise" in their ears and have sought medical help to get rid of this nuisance! The medical profession cannot explain what it is but gives it a name – tinnitus, without even being able to provide any real meaningful treatment. It is claimed to have multiple causes and a variety of helpful suppression devices are prescribed. A whole industry has grown up around helping those afflicted with this mysterious illness. However, in the majority of instances, it is neither a physical or psychological ailment but the expression of the cosmic sound vibration within our consciousness. There may be rare instances where it is really an illness, but it is rare indeed.

Those who are suffering from this malady would do well to consider refining their body-mind complex to attune to the sounds instead of partaking of harmful drugs. The sounds may be a clarion call to take up meditation.

The true inner sounds are called anahata or "unstruck" or uncaused to differentiate them from normal sounds or even higher vibrations which are caused by the effect of one physical object striking against another physical object. That inner sound that the yogis listen to is called nada or the divine flow. We can experience this nada as a flute sound, a roaring river or thunder, sound of crickets or electricity as well as other variations such as spontaneous sounds that can be interpreted in human language. Nada can have many degrees of manifestation depending on the level that is accessed.

At the cosmic level, nada is called para [that is, para-nada] and it is to this level that aspiring seekers hope to reach. This plane of existence is called the causal plane. At the next lower level nada is called pashyanti it is a mental vibration that corresponds to the mental plane. This is followed by the nada of the madhyama, that is a whispering or mental recitation, vibrating from the astral worlds. Finally, nada takes on the gross form of the spoken word in the physical world.

As the yogis followed this nada to its ultimate point or bindu, they experienced the state of Shiva-Shakti or pure consciousness vibrating with energy, a state that transcended time and space. From their shared experience, these yogis formulated their evolutionary model in which nada is the first evolute to emerge from Shiva-Shakti and bindu is the nucleus that holds this vibration.

# Kriya Yoga and Nada

There is a close connection between the evolutionary yogic techniques of Kriya Yoga and the little known system of spiritual development called Nada Yoga. In the Kriya system, there are a series of techniques called Omkar Kriyas which involve listening to the sound vibrations of Om. Also, an advanced technique called Jyoti Mudra which requires both the vibrations of light and sound. These parts of Kriya Yoga are an integration of the light sound techniques of Nada Yoga.

The authority for Nada Yoga goes back to antiquity, to the most revered spiritual texts called the Upanishads. There are 108 recognized Upanishads, some dating back to 1000 BCE. The Nada-Bindu Upanishad gives a thorough foundation for the system of Nada:

> *Seated in the yogic perfect pose*
> *With aid of Vaishnavi-mudra practice*
> *Be absorbed in the inner sound from the right ear*
> (Verse 31)

To the modern spiritual practitioner, it may appear that Nada Yoga doesn't seem to be mentioned much and its lineage vanished. However, the truth is that it has been incorporated and absorbed into most of the modern spiritual yoga lineages and forms the basis of a few modern groups under different labels.

The practice variously called jyoti-mudra, shambavi mudra or yoni mudra plays an important role in Kriya, Tantra, Hatha, Laya, Kundalini and Shabda yogas, as well in the lineages of the Kabir Panth and Radhasoamis.

Consider a quote from the 8th century spiritual giant Shankaracharya: 'With a calm mind and abandoning all thoughts, meditate upon Nada if you desire to attain perfection in Yoga.' Or one from the Shiva Samhita, a Hatha Yoga treatise: 'The best posture is the perfect pose, the best way to cultivate strength is by holding of breath, the best energetic seal is the Kechari Mudra, and the best way to dissolve the mind is by Nada."

There is a basic difference in polarity between Mantra and Nada, although eventually, they lead to the same point. In mantra, the practitioner repeats a set of sounds that have the power to calm the mind and lead to higher consciousness. In Nada, there is a mode of listening and being absorbed in the inner, "unstruck sounds", a witnessing and detachment from all mental processes. In Mantra yoga, in the active repetition of the mantra, there is also a process of becoming passively absorbed in its vibration. Therefore, in reality, both are active-passive but from different poles.

In Nada, we see the vibration of light – the bindu point, before becoming absorbed in the para-nada of cosmic consciousness. This is an important part of the practice of Kriya Yoga.

# Stages of Spiritual Practice

When we talk about sadhana or spiritual practice, most often we highlight the techniques and the progress in proficiency of practice. We might give tips on how to practice better or guidelines to overcome certain obstacles that will occur along the path.

However, it may be instructive to examine the psychological stages that a spiritual practitioner will go through once he or she starts on the path, irrespective of the particular path or techniques. This can be helpful to put oneself in perspective and also help understand why we observe certain characteristics from someone at certain times and the behavior changes.

A dominant characteristic of someone who has recently started a spiritual practice is the need for information from the community or from a teacher / Master. The principle psychological need is for external validation of one's chosen path. The practitioner is in a cocoon of joy when at last having been established in an evolutionary journey but still harbor doubts and the mind seeks to alleviate concerns through as much information as possible from the internet, fellow practitioners, books, and teachers to make sure that the techniques are being practiced correctly and remove any doubts about the path. This is a necessary stage but when prolonged, may indicate incompatibility with the particular practice or path.

When the practitioner becomes proficient and established in her sadhana, her focus shifts to her physical, astral or mental experiences. He becomes engrossed in the visions, dreams or flashes of intuition that arises in the course of the practice. This is a dangerous phase because it can lead to dependence on experiences that are inconsistent and often non reproducible. When some insights turn out well, one is in ecstasy and feels validated but when they fail, one is depressed and doubt the effort put into one's practice. It is important to let go of such external experiences in order to make progress.

At the third stage, the practitioner no longer concerns herself with external experiences or psychic gifts. He is joyful in the practice itself. He would sooner give up eating or sleeping then miss his daily practice. She knows that the purpose of her sadhana is spiritual transformation and can observe the changes to her thoughts, words and deeds as a result of the transformation. At this stage, the practitioner is truly established and will not be shaken to give up his chosen path. All that is required is regularity, perseverance and the divine grace for a long life to finish the path.

# Follow the Higher Path

In key spiritual texts, re-birth and liberation are explained in terms of the moon and the Sun, keeping in mind that we are not talking about the physical sun and moon but the existential planes they represent. If a person has done a lot of good deeds, such that the good exceeds the bad, then such a person will go to the moon after passing and enjoying the nectar of the gods or *pitris* (forefathers). When the momentum of the good deeds gets exhausted, there will be a coming back from the heavenly plane, to rebirth into this world. The good deeds have taken the soul to the *Chandraloka* and it enjoyed blissful experience there and after the exhaustion of the blissful experience there, subsequent to the exhaustion of the momentum of those deeds, there is a reversal, a coming back. The five elements will then form a new body vehicle, according to the balance of *Karma*. Rebirth is certain for those who only cultivate good actions such as charity and good works.

For those who have practiced yoga, or have otherwise walked the spiritual path, they are destined to go to the heart of the sun. Highly purified souls bright in their behavior, shining in their character, travel through the rays of the sun to the orb of the sun. The rays of the sun are the paths through which the soul travels higher and reaches the solar plane. In order to go to the sun, the soul has to be bright, powerful, and purified. The soul gets further liberated in the solar plane through guidance and practice, and do not have to return to earth for rebirth.

One's *sadhana* or spiritual practice is critical because one day or the other, by the power of your practice and the grace of the divine, you will go to the solar plane, provided you are determined to attain *moksha* or liberation. This is important to understand, because if a spiritual practitioner does not become Self-Realized in his or her life-time, there are several options available depending on the level of achievement – returning to the physical plane for further practice or going on to the solar plane for higher practice.

When one has graduated from the solar plane, it opens up to higher stages of ascent. There is no sudden jump into the Supreme Being. The soul crosses through the worlds above, the five elements, the physical embodiment of the fourteen worlds - *Bhu-loka* up to *Satya-loka*, and eventually, towards the Universal Being, - *Brahma-loka*. The consciousness of individuality is maintained as needed for compassion and love. The nearer you go to the border of the Universal Being, the less you become conscious of your individuality. Yet the individuality in a very rarefied form persists. At that time, says the texts say that the manifest Divine sends a messenger, a being of light comes and leads the soul along the path towards the un-manifest and absolute Being.. This is the stage of cosmic consciousness but it is still not complete liberation, because to have cosmic consciousness there must be some object of which one must be conscious. The process by which complete liberation is achieved is the mystery between the Supreme and the *yogi*. We cannot understand nor speculate beyond a certain point.

*Sadhana* is the pathway to liberation. The spiritual guide shows the way and gives the spiritual push to start the engine of achievement. The power of liberation is by the purity of your purpose and intention, and the expansion of your love to all beings. Cultivation of the Love

Principle provides the fuel that will propel you on the path. This is because even though the Divine has no attributes and cannot be belittled by our mental conceptual framework, we can only conceive of the Divine with attributes. We, as human beings, can think only as human beings even in respect of the absolute. We think of the vast dimensions of the comprehension of God's Existence, in terms of superlatives, such as 'All-mighty', 'All-knowing', All-powerful', 'All-Loving', 'All-blissful'. These are the characteristics that we are able to conceive and attribute to the Divine. However, the one accessible attribute that we can all agree on is "All-Loving" and therefore, this is the one attribute that we can develop along the higher path.

**Figure 8**
*Life & Living*
*The Intentional Life Model*

# Is Sex an Impediment on the Spiritual Path?

This is one of the more frequently asked questions that I'm emailed about and it seems to be at the root cause of a lot of stress among spiritual seekers.

In the history of humanity's spiritual efforts there has always been an ambivalent attitude towards one of the most basic instinct and pre-occupation of human beings. The sexual instinct is the animal urge for the survival of our species while the pre-occupation with the sexual act is conditioned by the gratification of sensual pleasure and consummation of emotional love.

How then did it get such a bad rap? At the root of our attitudes is the realization that the life-force and energy required and released during sex is the most powerful force that can be accessed by normal men and women. In the ancient mysteries and religions of the West, there were actually ceremonies and festivals which sought to harness these energies under controlled conditions and for higher purposes. However, over time these practices degenerated into merely gratifications of pleasures and resulted in newer religions which sought to control the energy by making sex into a sin in fact if not in name. The rise of Christianity and Islam has burdened humanity with a major guilt trip, including the popular misconception that Adam and Eve got kicked out of Paradise because they had sex and St. Augustine somehow related his concept of original sin to sex as well. The current status is that sex and spirituality seems to be contradictory and celibacy a requirement for a truly religious or spiritual person – priest, monks, nuns etc.

In the East, during ancient times, all the great spiritual Masters were married householders with children and demonstrated that sex was not an impediment. However, during the advent of the minor Kali Yuga or materialistic age around 600 BCE, there was a movement to harness the sexual energy for spiritual purposes by emphasizing celibacy. This led to the founding of first the Buddhist monastic order and later to Hindu swamis. The premise then was that householders could not be serious about the spiritual path. The emphasis was the saving of the energy which would somehow be used to speed up spiritual evolution.

Naturally, not long after occurred the counter-trend to utilize the sexual act itself which led to the rise of Tantra. This has given rise to an absurd amount of confusion for spiritual seekers over the last two thousand years and Sexual Tantra has become a major trend among the pleasure seekers in the West.

My purpose in going over this historical outline is to two-fold: it shows that our attitudes toward sex shifts and changes over time and in different cultures and also that provides a foundation for how the attitudes can affect our spiritual life.

To wrap up the outline, I wish to point out that we finished the minor Kali Yuga in 1800 CE and are now in the Dwapara Yuga, a somewhat more enlightened era. In 1862, the immortal Babaji initiated a householder into the sacred science of Kriya Yoga – Lahiri Mahasaya went on to sire children even after his initiation and becoming a Master, to demonstrate that sex itself is not an impediment to spiritual attainment.

However, his enlightened teaching which matches those of the ancient Rishis is to utilize as much of your energy, including sexual energy in one's practice, as possible. Engage in marital sex if there is a need or duty or if one feels the desire, especially for procreation. This is no different than if one is hungry or thirsty, one should eat or drink. Sex is a natural part of our human and animal heritage. Eventually, by the persevering practice of Yoga, the spiritual seeker attains to Realization in which his/her energy system is wholly and totally harmonized and under effortless control in all activities – there is no separation into material or spiritual anymore.

There is the danger that some neophytes try to integrate their spiritual practice into their sexual activities in the hope that this will speed up

*Rudra Shivananda*

their progress. However, this is almost always a big trap as there is hardly anyone who is not a Master who can maintain the necessary self-control in the midst of sensual and sexual activity. The trap is that the instead of overcoming the attraction and attachment to the five senses, the seeker justifies indulgence in the name of spirituality becomes more and more attached to the five senses. The theoretical logic of sexual tantra breaks down in the practical sphere of sensual gratification.

One should also keep in mind that much of the Tantric literature, the right-hand path, is concerned with meditative activity utilizing the emotions and released energies for spiritual purposes through transformation – there is no actual sexual activity, apart from the male and female energies within oneself.

I'm not saying that sexual tantra is all wrong, but a Tantric Master may be more difficult to find that anyone realizes. Therefore, my recommendation is that one should engage in spiritual practice and sexual activities separately and let them have their own sphere. It is easier to bring the fruits of one's realization into different spheres such as work, family and sex, social activity etc, as one's consciousness is raised. The important point is to relinquish any guilt associated with sexual activity or any doubts about the attainment of higher consciousness while still engaged in worldly activities. Don't let the left-over lower consciousness of the Kali Yuga affect your spiritual progress.

*[168]*

# Sexual Orientation and Spirituality

Yogic spirituality is not a religion and does not pass any judgment on the spectrum of human behavior. I'm often asked by spiritual seekers with different sexual orientations about whether it is a factor on the spiritual path or whether there is any impact on their practice.

Sexual orientation is a complex of emotional, physical and mental needs and is not a subject that is discussed in yogic texts, which are revealing the modes and paths for transcending the human condition as such. Whether a person is straights or gay is immaterial for real yogis since these are all conditions which are concerning our bondage to the material world.

Society and those religions which form the basis of societies tend to value heterosexual behavior because of the need to propagate the family unit, to further the spread of their population. In their world-view, there would be no place for alternative sexual orientations.

In the yogic perspective, gender and all physical attributes as well as emotional and mental conditionings are a matter of previous *karma* being played out in this life-time. A physical body has a primary male or female condition while the emotional and mental aspects are a mix of both – that is why you can have a nurturing father or a dominating mother. This interplay of male and female attributes such as the left and right brain game is psychologically acceptable and understandable.

Since the Self that we wish to realize as our true nature does not have a gender and does not engage in procreation, paths of Self-Realization take an agnostic stand on these aspects. This does not mean that there are not so-called yogis who take unreasonable stands in the name of spirituality. Some are even against women being able to achieve liberation without being reborn as a man first! This in spite of their worshipping and praying to the Divine Mother. Some yogis have also condemned the gay life-style without explanation because of their religious upbringing. Unfortunately, this is the current state of yogic teachers – a microcosm of society.

Lots of negative energy that can impede a gay spiritual seeker – both from others and also due to guilt feelings programmed into them by their elders. These negative energies and emotions need to be transformed into positive energy through special practices.

The practices of yoga are not affected by sexual orientation as such but more by the display of self-control or lack thereof. Most yogic practices require *prana* or life-force energy and so it is necessary to preserve one's sexual energy in order to fuel the practices, especially if one is on the path to raise the *kundalini* energy. Excessive loss of sexual energy will result in a lack of the *prana* needed. A balanced life-style is the key whether one is straight or gay.

In summary, sexual orientation play little if any part in yogic sadhana and does not significantly impact the path of Self-Realization.

# A Lesson for Shankaracharya

One of the great Masters of Yoga was Adi-Shankaracharya who was born realized and was commanded by his Guru, Govindapada to go to Benares at the age of twelve to teach. By the age of thirty, Shankaracharya had become the greatest Master of time. He had reformed Hinduism and setup major spiritual centers in the four corners of India as well as defeated all the major Buddhist and Jain leaders in debates – no one could withstand his brilliance.

Finally, he decided to challenge Mandana Mishra to a debate.

Mandana was already aged, perhaps seventy years old and been undefeated during that time. Whoever loses would have to become the disciple of the other and since both of them had thousands upon thousands of followers, they would also have to come under the winner's umbrella.

Now, in order to decide who had won the debate, a judge had to be found and Shankaracharya decided to ask Mandana's wife Bharati to be the judge since she was also renowned for her great wisdom. After weeks of debate on all spiritual aspects, Bharati declared the young Shankaracharya as winner. However, she also declared that since she was the better half of Mandana, he had only half lost and that the young acharya would need to defeat her as well for a full win.

Reluctantly, Shankaracharya agreed and asked Mandana to be the judge. Now, Bharati knew after the weeks of debates that there was very little under the Sun that she could challenge the young Master on but she had identified a weakness and so she pursued the topic of sex. This perplexed Shankaracharya because he had always been celibate and had no knowledge of the subject. Therefore he asked for an adjournment of forty days. He then asked his disciples to find out if any royal personage had recently passed away because he had decided to enter another body in order to find out more about sex and what better body to use than a king's!

The disciples found that a nearby king had passed away that very day and Shankaracharya went into a cave to meditate. He asked his students to take good care of his body and also gave special instructions to his chief disciple to go get him if he had not returned to his own body within the set time. Then he left his own body and entered that of the king and enjoyed the delights of sex. However, after some weeks, he began to forget who he had been and became immersed in his role and enamored of the king's life.
At the set date, the disciple came to the king's court to tell him to return to his own body by reminding him of the debate he was having with the lady Bharati but the king could not remember. Finally, the

disciple gave a discourse on the Shankaracharya's teachings and this woke him from his slumber and he immediately returned to his body. He then went back to the debate and answered all of Bharati's questions to her satisfaction and she declared him the winner.

As he returned to his students, the great acharya gave a discourse on the dangers of sensual gratification on the spiritual path – it can make even a renunciate forget his realization. He also declared that if a householder can achieve Self-Realization, it was a greater achievement than for a monk to do so!

# Higher Consciousness for Peace

Spiritual seekers have certain definable goals generally in the order of liberation, freedom from suffering or Self-Realization – all of which would require a dramatic shift into higher strata of super-conscious states. How long the path will take is highly variable depending on the strength of practice, the power of the path, the karmic obstacles, and grace of the spiritual guide.

It is important to understand that the spiritual path is not one where you either win or lose and that there is a continuum of achievement. In fact I would say that it may be more important for world peace if the general population raised their consciousness by an order of magnitude than if only a few people achieved Self-Realization. Of course, if a few enlightened people became guides for the others, then the process would be quickened tremendously.

The goal then becomes the uplifting of human consciousness. In the larger sense, this goal is the mission of great beings such as Babaji and his helpers. This may also be part of the drama to be played out in 2012 and for many more years to come.

From a practical point of view, even a little of the beginner's practice such as those of popular yoga postures can have a profound effect in the behavior of the practitioners. Awareness of one's body and mind helps us to understand better our reaction patterns and break-up childhood and cultural habit patterns – this leads to a greater openness and tolerance for the perspectives of others.

Meditation practice can help to control and overcome many emotional compulsions leading to healthier attitudes. Toxic emotions such as anger, fear and lust can be as easily transmitted as the common cold and lead to much greater damage, unless one is inoculated by mental control. So much of the world's ills have been due to uncontrolled emotions – genocides and wars could have been stopped if enough people refused to be caught up in them.

Proper breathing practice and control of life-force brings about better overall health and breaks all types of conditionings. The lack of energy leads to fatigue which in turn predisposes one to accept old thoughts and patterns – an unquestioning and lazy attitude – apathy that allows all types of negativity to continue. An abundance of life-force is necessary for happiness.

Higher consciousness is all about greater awareness of one's thoughts, words and actions and the willingness to control them according to universal ethics and values.

If more people gave due consideration to their thoughts, there would be less pollution of the thought waves throughout the world – it is difficult for us to remain calm and positive when we are swimming in an ocean of negative thought waves. If more people started generating positive thoughts of love and compassion, this will counteract the thoughts of anger and hatred. If we can train more and more people to be calm and happy under adverse conditions – that is raising their consciousness, then there will be less confrontation and more peace – it takes two sides to make a fight.

There are plenty of opportunities for those spiritual seekers on the path who have achieved a measure of self-control and emotional steadiness to help those around them to overcome intolerance, emotional turmoil, and mental laziness. It is not necessary to wait until one is Self-realized before participating in the uplifting of world consciousness. This does not mean that one should pronounce oneself a teacher or even Master before one's time but one can certainly put one's effort to good use without assuming lofty titles. This is the work for higher consciousness that will have a far-reaching effect in future generations.

# Spiritual Art

I've always been attracted to the various ways that the great saints and sages have tried to express their higher consciousness to us, from spiritual poetry to philosophical writings or in music and also in art.

Poetic imagery is a great medium of expression but is limited by language – I may not understand the language used by the sage and translations lose much of the potency of the original. It seems that art forms can overcome these language barriers.

Art is a means of expressing our nature and identity, of our creativity, of our pains and pleasures, of our knowledge and ignorance and of our fears and desires. When an artist taps into her higher consciousness, she can help others understand different aspects of reality which are not susceptible to ordinary consciousness. Art has to find resonance within the perceiver to be meaningful. Sometimes, the artist herself may not be consciously aware of the deeper dimensions of her own work and how it will speak to those who admire it.

Throughout history, human beings have strived to express their understanding and aspirations in works of art. Only those which were cast in durable forms have survived to our times – those in stone, clay or bone, or the frescoes on walls. Last year, I was fascinated with the great stone images and wall paintings when I visited the Ellora and Ajanta caves in the India – they had spiritual art from the 3rd century to the 9th century, from gigantic stone temple art or huge stone Buddhas to delicate and beautiful paintings. A few months ago, I visited the London Museum again and there was an exhibit of spiritual art from India, Tibet, Nepal, Cambodia and Thailand in one of the halls. Aside from the sublime and awesome visual impact, I was struck by the evident investment of humanity's time, effort and resources in even this small selection of works. Sometimes an artist would spend years to create a particular work – whether the peaceful and sublime form of a Buddha or the whirling movement of a dancing Shiva or the lovingness of Jesus.

In the past, a master artist would only spend her time and effort on some worthwhile project because of limited resources and in almost all cases, their subjects were primarily spiritual or religious, or both. Only in the last couple of hundred years has there started a trend towards self-expression and so we might be led into thinking that there is a movement away from spiritual art. Indeed, from about fifty years ago, there has been a movement towards commercial art – works that have mass appeal and merely have superficial meaning if any – not much better than bill-boards! This trend towards commercial art is understandable, after all, the artist needs to live and has to pay bills and if she tries to express something deeper, it might not sell.

There are artists who claim to be in a category called spiritual art. However, they may primarily be commercial also, just another way to sell themselves. After all, an artist should understand that she is expressing the spirit in every piece of work, whether it is in representation form or an abstract piece. There should ideally be no such thing as non-spiritual art.

There is much to be said for the use of abstract art to express spiritual reality. Immediately, we are struck by the use of colors, curves and lines and geometry. Our pre-conceptions are challenged – there are no comfortable and recognizable forms for us to stick to and we must connect in a deeper and formerly unknown zone.

Those who have kept to representational forms have also discovered new ways of challenging our pre-conceptions by capturing and combining forms in new ways, from the grotesque to the sublime, from beauty to the disgusting, from courage to fear, from religious to irreligious – all knocking us from our comfort zone so that we can re-examine ourselves and make new connections. This is a very important part of spirituality.

It strikes me that sometimes when I look at some modern works of art, I wonder if the artist is aware of the intrinsic impact of colors in his work. Even if we forget about the subject matter and the form of the artwork, the very colors used can have a strong effect on the viewer. It is because the energy centers within our subtle body – the whirling lotuses or wheels of pranic energy called chakras are affected by different color vibrations. These chakras are responsible for our health as well as the opening to higher consciousness – they are responsible for our health because they control the life-force sent to our organs and cells and they help in our spiritual evolution because they enable the raising of our higher consciousness energy called kundalini. Certain color combinations inhibit the proper functioning of the chakras while others can enhance them. This is part of the reason for the attraction of certain pieces of art. However, just as some people are attracted to horror movies, some people are attracted to art whose colors are detrimental to their well-being or spiritual progress.

I hope that artists will be more attuned to the use of colors in their work and be responsible to ensure the health and spiritual impact of these colors. I hope that artists will connect with their deeper and higher selves and express themselves to give us spiritual works of wonder and joy and help us to understand hidden aspects of reality.

# What are you listening to?

It is surprising that most of us spend very little time considering with what kinds of sounds we bombard our sense of hearing. We probably spend more time on what we eat and what we wear. There is less awareness of the impact of sounds, such as music and songs to our well-being. Those on the spiritual path need to take extra care because of the impact of sounds our subtle bodies and life-force energy.

Of course, you will say that we have likes and dislikes as far as music and songs are concerned and that many of us spend significant time shopping around or downloading our favorites for listening. However, just as with food, we may like something that is bad for us, judging our audio selection based on attachment is not particularly worthwhile. But is there any harm?

We need to be aware that since all sounds are vibrations and these vibrations have been shown to affect the very molecules of our bodies – consider the experiments of a Japanese scientist on the effect of various words on water molecule … positive words make beautiful and symmetrical crystal patterns while negative words make grotesque and misshapen patterns… our bodies are 70% water. On a yogic perspective, we would consider the mantric properties of all sounds including words and music. These vibrations affect the chakras or energy centers in the subtle body and since these chakras affect the distribution of life-force or prana to the physical, emotional and mental bodies as well, the vibrations affect all levels of our being. If a particular sound pattern affects the heart center positively, it would heal physical heart maladies and evoke the emotion of love while another sound pattern might harm the heart and evoke the emotion of hatred. Unfortunately, the music of most popular songs stimulates the first and second chakras while their words negatively affect the heart or throat centers.

Classical Indian musicians are quite aware of the affect of the sounds on our well-being, emotions and thought patterns. Certain music patterns evoke patriotic feelings while others cause sadness – this is the science of the ragas. Each note of the musical scale affects one of the chakras more than the others – there are seven notes, one for each chakra. In addition, each chakra is resonant with certain consonants and vowels more than others and so we can actually analyze how certain sounds and words will affect the chakras. Unfortunately, it is a hit-and-miss for modern musicians and song writers and they have no clue about what they are doing to their listeners, who in turn are blind to the serious damage than can be done to them – it is like taking a slow poison.

Not everyone would like to listen to classical Indian music or spiritual chants all the time and so we should exercise our discrimination in determining the affect of contemporary songs and music. Even for those that we like, we need to become aware of how they affect our physical, energetic, emotional and mental well-being – there can be long-term damage that will impede our spiritual progress.

# Harness Creativity At Will

Whether you are a creative in the traditional sense of being an artist, musician and writer, or need to apply creativity into solving your problems such as a programmer or marketer, we can learn to harness our powers of creativity better with yogic techniques.

One of the easiest ways is to change the active brain lobe at will using breathing techniques. The right brain is correlated with higher inspiration and creativity and the right brain is connected with activity of the left nostril. It has been well known for thousands of years that our nostrils are not always both opened fully at the same time – one nostril is usually more open than the other and this changes every few hours. It has been discovered that when the left nostril is more opened, there is more activity on the right brain. Therefore, if you find that your right nostril is more opened and you need to harness your creativity rather than your rational, analytical powers, you should change the dominant nostril to the left side – close your right nostril with the right index finger and breathe only through the left nostril for about 15 minutes. This forced left nostril breathing will activate the right brain activity.

Another method is to utilize the harmonic vibration from one of the creativity mantras of Saraswati, who is the cosmic creative power and can be accessed for our microcosmic activities. The following is a Saraswati stotra which is chanted aloud:

**Ya kundendu tushaar haara dhavalaa, ya shubra vastraavrutaa**
**Ya veenavara danda manditakaraa, ya shweta padmaasana**
**Ya brahamaachyuta shankara prabhrutibhi: Devyai sadaa vanditaa**
**Saamaan paatu Saraswati bhagawati, ni:shesha jaadyaa pahaa.**

*O godess Saraswati, pure and radiant as the full moon and the frost, wearing a garland of jasmine flowers in the your white*

*robes, seated on your lotus throne; with the veena on your lap;*
*O one from whom has originated the three, Brahma, Vishnu and*
*Shankara, O one, who is surrounded and respected by all gods,*
*may you bless and protect me and remove every vestige of laziness*
*and sloth from inside me.*

This mantra should be chanted at least 27 times before undertaking
any creative efforts. Those who undertake creative work at all times,
usually chant this mantra 108 times every morning.

# Yoga is not Fool-proof

There is a popular misrepresentation that yoga is easy and anyone
can do it. This is certainly not the case for the higher practices
associated with the spiritual paths of yoga and is not even the case
for the simple asanas (physical postures) which form the preparatory
phase of Hatha Yoga.

There has been a proliferation of physical posture systems under the
universal umbrella of yoga. Everyday, millions of people go to their
neighborhood yoga studio and strain themselves to be more flexible,
burn some fat or release some stress. Most of these novices are
not aware that the yoga systems that they are made to practice are
formulated by gymnasts, ballet dancers or exercise enthusiasts, who
have twisted the traditional postures to suit their own predispositions
or commercial goals. They have also brought with them a competitive
flavor which has no place in the traditional understanding of asanas
– I wish they would call it something different than yoga Olympics!
The competitive flavor permeates the studio practice even though a
well-meaning instructor may downplay or caution the students – it

gets ingrained in each and every posture as there is an ideal form and pace that is imposed. This has caused the frequent occurrence of "yoga injuries", most minor but some serious.

Most of the new Western systems and even modern representations of Indian systems have moved away from the goals of steadiness and health that the founders of Hatha Yoga had envisioned for the asanas. Instead, the focus is now on performance and some ideal form in the mind of the posture leaders. The student has to align herself in a particular way despite the large variances in body sizes and forms.

In keeping with the high physical demands of the current posture systems, it is necessary for the average fit person, not to mention those who are struggling with their physical aspects, to prepare before getting into a posture class. One should talk candidly with the instructor and understand thoroughly the physical requirements, however gentle they may be. Only after careful consideration and examination of your current physical state, the requirements of the system and the capability of the instructor, should one take a class. Make sure that you can feel comfortable that the instructor is concerned for your well-being, unless you are one of those who go to a yoga class to feel the burn and get pushed beyond your limit! My cautionary note is not for one who likes to take extra risks in everything.

A posture class should always start with extensive warm-up of all major muscle groups and joints – even experienced practitioners can hurt themselves going in cold. It is best not to take part in a mixed class of various levels of practitioners as it is not possible for an instructor to monitor your progress in such an environment. It is your responsibility to be in touch with your physical state and have sufficient awareness of your limits at any particular moment in time. Our bodies have a variance in flexibility on different days due to the tensions and stress that we may be subjected to. It is should not be goal to practice through major discomfort and pain. I repeat, don't practice when in pain.

With proper attention, most posture related injuries can be prevented.

Less noticeable are the problems caused by the malpractice of breathing techniques. Changing one's breathing pattern can cause powerful changes in emotions and mental processes. However, the practice of breath retention can cause major physical problems and should only be taught to advanced students under expert supervision.

It may surprise you to learn that even meditation practices can cause problems for those who are not prepared. There is a graded series of meditative steps that need to be followed. Jumping into higher meditations with a confused or unstable mind is not recommended. Serious emotional and mental injuries can occur for those who take up powerful techniques that are meant to transform one's consciousness without proper preparation or understanding of the consequences.

Human nature has not changed so significantly since the sages laid down the rules and formulated the proper and graded Yoga systems that modern men and women can ignore them. There is a propensity for spiritual seekers to assume that they can skip all the preliminary steps that are meant to prepare them for the higher practices and just go straight to these sacred techniques that are now widely available from varied sources. This has led to a lack of progress in the best cases and emotional and mental disruptions in severe cases.

My intention is not to dissuade the sincere practitioner from pursuing their paths with vigor but only to sound a healthy warning, whether you are a casual posture student or a serious sadhak. Preparation is the one of the keys to success on the spiritual paths of Yoga.

# The Three Puppet Strings

In yogic philosophy, all matter in the universe arises from the fundamental substrate called prakriti. From prakriti arises the three primary gunas or qualities that create the essential aspects of all nature—energy, matter and consciousness. These three gunas are tamas (darkness), rajas (activity), and sattva (lightness). All three gunas are always present in all beings and objects but vary in their relative amounts leading to various levels of material attachment and delusion.

Lord Krishna has said (BG 14:05 – 14:08):

The eternal embodied soul to the material body bound
The three-fold principle binding mind is found

Pure and good, illuminating sattva snare
Attachment to happiness and knowledge beware

Restless and passionate, intense selfish rajas craving
Attachment to desire borne on fruits of work saving

Ignorant and lazy, tamas delusion inducing wrap
Attachment to negligence and non-action soul trap

Understanding the gunas is critical to knowledge of human psychology. The mind is highly unstable and fluctuates under the changing dominance of the different gunas. The temporarily dominate guna acts like a lens that effects our perceptions and perspective of the world. When the mind is dominated by rajas it will experience world events as chaotic activity and it will react in a passionate and restless manner.

Yoga teaches that we have the ability to consciously alter the levels of the gunas in our bodies and minds. The gunas cannot be separated or removed in oneself, but can be consciously acted upon to encourage their increase or decrease. A guna can be increased or decreased through the interaction and influence of external objects, lifestyle practices and thoughts.

An important way to regulate these gunas in body and mind is through ayurvedic cooking which seeks to increase the sattvic, decrease rajasic and avoid the tamasic foods.

Sattvic foods are fresh, juicy, light, nourishing, sweet and tasty and give the necessary energy to the body without taxing it. It is the foundation of higher states of consciousness. Examples are juicy fruits, fresh vegetables that are easily digestible, fresh milk and butter, whole soaked or sprouted beans, grains and nuts, many herbs and spices in the right combinations with other foods.

Rajasic foods are bitter, sour, salty, pungent, hot and dry. They increase the speed and excitation of the nervous system and chaotic thoughts in the mind. It is the foundation of motion, activity and pain. Examples are sattvic foods that have been overcooked or oil-fried, foods and spices that are strongly exciting such as garlic and onions.

Tamasic foods are dry, old and decaying. They consume large amounts of energy while being digested. They are the foundation of ignorance, doubt, pessimism. Examples are foods that have been strongly processed, canned or frozen and/or are old, stale or incompatible with each other - meat, fish, eggs and liquor are especially tamasic.

Saints and seers can survive easily on sattvic foods alone but householders living in the world and have to keep pace with its changes also need rajasic energy. It is necessary to keep a balance as much as possible.

Since all gunas create attachment and thus bind one's self to the ego, it is necessary to transcend them. While the seeker should initially cultivate sattva, his/her ultimate goal is to transcend their misidentification of the self with the gunas and to be unattached to both the good and the bad, the positive and negative qualities of all life.

**When one rises above the three gunas that originate in the body; one is freed from birth, old age, disease, and death; and attains enlightenment.** (BG 14:20).

# Take Time for Tea Now

Our minds become preoccupied with problems and accumulate stress without awareness of it even happening. I find that most people are suffering from a stress that slowly saps their will and their ability to live happily.

Stress is caused by worries of all sorts, such as about the future, the unknown, one's finances, one's relationships, one's job security and a myriad of other things. Each of these emotional and mental stressors causes physical tension in one's body which, if not released quickly, accumulates and becomes chronic. This chronic tension leads to fatigue and inability to sleep or relax that in turn leads to greater stress in a vicious cycle.

We can release the physical tension through exercise or relaxation techniques but it recurs because the underlying stress is still present. One needs to break the pattern of stress formation, and this can be done through meditation and breathing techniques. However, paradoxically, those who are under the greatest stress "do not have time" or are "too tired" to perform the techniques that can save them from the actual cause of their fatigue and inability to focus.

A practical and effective solution is to take time for a cup of tea! Consider the merits of the Japanese tea ceremony – concentration on the moment and integrating body and mind. Although I'm not suggesting anything so ritualistic or complex, the key to breaking stress is to take the mind off the thoughts which tend to be repeating over and over again the same patterns of distress. Any activity that engages all five senses can work but I find that a fifteen minute tea break can produce much of the benefits of hours of relaxation. Coffee does not provide the same result due to the higher caffeine content which induces hyperactivity and stimulation of the mind. The best is herbal tea, but even normal green or black tea can be used.

Choose tea that has a strong and pleasing aroma. Use tea leaves or even flower teas such as orange blossom rather than the tea bag. While the water is boiling, mentally repeat the following:

*I am free from stress and worries*
*I am calm and contented*
*I am at peace in body and mind*

Pour the hot water over the tea leaves and let it sit for two minutes. Watch the tea leaves settling and reacting to the water. Strain the tea leaves and pour your tea into a cup. Inhale the tea deeply several times. Put your right hand about half an inch over the cup and feel the steamy heat while repeating aloud for a minute or two, "Om shanti". When it is possible, try to sip the tea and feel the taste on your tongue and aroma when you inhale as you slowly drink, keeping awareness of your joy in the experience.

Take at least fifteen minutes. The best times are late afternoon and early evening. It is also good to try it in the morning when you have less stress and it is easier to perform this yogic tea ceremony for stress release.

# The Heart Center

The Anahata Chakra or heart center is the seat of human consciousness. It is the center of transition from the animal consciousness of the three lower chakras to the divine consciousness of the higher three chakras. Most of humanity is still struggling and have their base at the navel center and often fall to the lower passionate animal consciousness of lust and fear. Those operating from the navel center are primarily concerned with controlling others and accumulating wealth and possessions. The Navel center is the seat of power, possessions and position or status.

The heart center is in the subtle life-force or energy body which overlays the physical body. It is located at the back around the area between the shoulder blades along the subtle central spinal energy channel called the sushumna nadi. It is the center that stores, transforms and transmits the life-force energy that keeps the physical heart and the circulatory system in good health.

It is also the seat of that part of the soul called the prana-atma of life-force soul. The mind or manas is based at the heart center. The primary positive emotion is love and the negative emotion is hatred. It is the center where we can transform our hatred into love. It is the degree to which we have developed our capacity of love that distinguishes a true human being from an animal. It is not enough that we love our children or spouse – that is something even some higher animals can accomplish – we need to extend our love to others to whom we have no family relationship, that is to friends and eventually even to strangers.

Reacting emotionally to events, situations and relationships is the mode of the navel center and is responsible for most of the problems of humanity. If we can move our consciousness to the loving mind of the heart center, we will act and react from the perspective of love and kindness. Development of the heart center is the key to earth peace.

The heart center also rules relationships and we can see how the world is mired in relationship problems because we cannot have a relationship of equality from the navel center. The navel center is of domination and submission. One party or the other will seek to dominate. A relationship can form when one party submits but it is not human nature to submit and there cannot be lasting peace in such a lop-sided relationship despite the literary pretensions of sado-masochistic psychology. If both parties try to exert dominance, then the relationship ends abruptly. A solid foundation for a healthy relationship requires mutual respect and with both parties trying to operate from the heart center.

We can develop our heart center and bring our consciousness to this base with the help of the appropriate yogic techniques and I teach a workshop for this purpose. However, even without such techniques, it is the power of awareness that can awaken the heart center. It is the awareness of love. It is the awareness of tolerance. It is the awareness of our egotistical and selfish desires. It is the awareness and willingness to look at a situation from someone else's perspective. It is awareness that can break through the barriers of the navel center and move us to the heart center.

The evolution towards higher consciousness begins when we take responsibility for seating ourselves in our loving heart center. It begins when we make the effort to act from the heart center. Peace begins when we operate from the heart center and if even a small portion of humanity activate their heart love, then there will be less and less violence and wars in this world.

# The Benefits of Shakti Healing

Everyone is constantly looking for the better or best healing methodology because we all get sick at some time or the other and we want to feel better all the time.

Some look to the modern medical infrastructure to get the newest wonder drug to eliminate whatever they are suffering from while others run after the latest alternative healing modality. Energy healing has become an important part of alternative remedies especially with the popularization of Reiki and Pranic Healing over the last 20 years.

I had experimented with various energetic healing systems and was working with other compassionate souls in the San Francisco area during the early 1990's to help those suffering from serious and terminal illnesses. Although we were able to help somewhat and ease the pain of many of those we visited, I was very dissatisfied with the overall lack of results from our healing efforts. The very few who were healed seemed to me to have done so from their own will and optimism and with minimal help from others. There was little correlation between our efforts and the resulting healing rate.

One of the limitations that I discovered early on was that the spiritual state of the healer had a strong impact on the amount of energy that could be channeled for healing. A spiritual practitioner who was initiated into various healing systems and taught the appropriate techniques seemed to be much more effective in energy healing than one who had no previous spiritual practice. This can be attributed to the more refined and expanded energy body of the practitioner.

A second limitation was the source of the energy. It was easily discovered that those who tried to use their own life-force or pranic energy would soon get exhausted versus those who were trying to channel the universal life force energy.

Another limitation that I encountered was that the ego-centric healer would often be ineffective and may actually pick up negative energy as a result of the healing attempt. Even though in most of the systems, the healer needs to put himself in a mode of being a channel for the universal energy, it was nearly impossible for him not to become involved emotionally or otherwise with the outcome of the healing. Dispassion does not come easily to a healer!

My search for a more effective healing system turned towards the Himalayan tradition of India from which most of the modern systems had directly or indirectly borrowed and in a strange turn, I discovered that my spiritual Master, Yogiraj Siddhanath, was also the Master of the ancient healing modalities of India. He has formulated a unique system called Shakti Healing based on these ancient techniques utilizing the energy of the Sun and of the Universal Mother.

It was immediately apparent that the Shakti system solved the energy source limitation because it was calling upon the highest energy source there is – the Cosmic Mother energy which is beyond all the other 6 levels of energy sources beginning with the personal prana. The Shakti energy is invoked by the power of ancient mantras in the divine Sanskrit language together with the appropriate yantras visualized as temporary gateway and receptacle.

The techniques in the Shakti system are powerful but easily learned, making them effective even for those without prior experience in such things. There are also a variety of techniques to target the physical, energetic, emotional, mental and karmic distress of the sufferer.

Another positive aspect of the Shakti system is the emphasis on self-healing versus healing others. This is a solution to the channeling limitation of someone who has not yet achieved Self-Realization. The greatest benefit from self-healing is that if someone who is suffering from a particular malady makes the effort to apply the techniques, the healing effect is multiplied many times! This is because the cause of all maladies is one's own bad Karma, which in turn is caused by one's own actions in the past. The most effective cure is therefore to overcome the Karmic cause by one's own healing actions in the present.

Even those who are not in distress in the present will benefit by practicing the self-healing techniques because they will remove the future cause of maladies – a preventive maintenance program.

# Developing a Grounded Practice

Today is Thanksgiving, a day to recognize all that we have to be thankful for. We give thanks to family and friends for their continuous support and to our various teachers for all that we have learned.

It is an opportune time to consider the gift of a spiritual practice that we may have been graced with by any spiritual teacher. Many sages have declared that a life is only worthwhile if one has had the good karma to be put on the path of spiritual evolution through the teachings of a true teacher.

The best thanks that any teacher can ask for is that his students can actualize his teachings. For spiritual instructions, an effective or firmly grounded practice called a sadhana is necessary to achieve the goals for higher consciousness. How then to develop such a practice?

According to Patanjali, "a practice has a firm ground when attended to for a long time, without interruption and with devotion to the truth."

First, it is taken for granted that success in a spiritual practice will require a significant amount of time – how long it takes can vary due to the intensity of individual effort as well as the individual karmic problems that need to be cleared. We do not start at the same spot like in a race – everyone starts at a different state and some will reach their goal sooner while others will reach a little later and therefore we need to give up any expectations of success within a set time-frame. We tend to get bored and lose interest when we have to do something over and over again for years – this is a great obstacle that has to be overcome. Remember that success may come in little steps or may come in large jumps depending on the type of path and amount of blockages.

Second, there needs to be continuity in the sadhana. A regular practice is more effective than one characterized by stoppages and intensive effort of short duration. Imagine what kind of result you would get by brushing your teeth every 7 days instead of every day. Even fifteen minutes or half an hour once every day is better than two or three hours of practice sporadically.

Finally, we need to be convinced that the practice can give the results desired – this is what is meant by being devoted to the truth. Before we start the sadhana, we need to have a basis for the faith that the practice actually will work – this comes from the given lineage of previous successful practitioners on the same path and from the example of the teacher as well. Without a foundation for the faith, it would be difficult to persevere for the many years of regular effort required.

Let us keep the words of Patanjali in mind as we give thanks for the spiritual grace that we have received, that we may keep alive the flame of sadhana within us during these difficult times.

# A Meditation For Christmas

Christmas is a time for celebration and also a time to commemorate the birth of a great spiritual Master and World Teacher - the Lord Jesus. Although from a purely historical perspective, December 25th is most probably not the date of Jesus's birth, it is one of the best day of the year to meditate and make spiritual progress by connecting with his power and blessing.

Let us meditate on one of the many deeper significances of this special time of year. It is the potential for the birth of Self-Realization in all sincere seekers. It is the path blazed by Master Jesus - the path of liberation from the cycle of death and suffering that we should celebrate as the true gospel of good tidings for all humanity. For sincere seekers, Christmas becomes a time to celebrate not only the birth of a Master, but the potential re-birth of all of us.

One of the symbols of Christmas is that of the Star that heralded the birth of Jesus. It is the Soul-Star that we will all perceive as we awaken to our true nature and in course of our Self-Realization. In the yogic mysteries, we are taught that when we are born, our soul-power is forced to scatter into the five sensory gateways of hearing, touch, sight, taste and smell. We then enter into a bondage to these sensory perceptions as our feelings, emotions and mental states become conditioned by them.

During our spiritual rebirth, we must reclaim our soul-power from the five senses and reconstitute our Soul-Star - the five-pointed star at our third-eye center - the star of Bethlehem.

Let us begin by siting in a quiet space with all the lights turned off and keeping the back straight but relaxed. Focus your attention on the incoming and outgoing breath in your nostrils for one or two minutes and then mentally repeat 'amen' twelve times after letting go of the breath. Move your attention to your tongue and concentrate there for a minute or two before mentally repeating 'amen' twelve times at the tongue. Then focus your attention on your eyes, feeling the eyeballs and the eye-lids for a few minutes before mentally repeating 'amen' twelve times there. For the sense of touch, we focus on the skin of our face, neck, hands and feet, mentally repeating 'amen' while concentrating on our skin. Finally, we bring our attention to our ears and the sense of hearing - repeat 'amen' twelve times. We have now purified the five sensory organs.

Focus your attention now on the third-eye center in the third-ventricle of the brain - midway between the mid-eyebrow and the back of the head. Mentally repeat ' amen' twelve times. Now, watch your breath as it enters and departs from your third-eye for at least five minutes. If you do not yet see a ball of light at the center, then visualize a five-pointed star there. As you inhale, visualize the star growing bigger and as you exhale, let it return to its own size.

This simple meditation will help us reform the soul-star that heralds the dawn of Christmas and the re-birth of Self-Realization. It is practised anyday to make that day into Christmas.

# Harness The Power of New Year

As we bid farewell to the hopes and fears of 2012 with more than a few sighs of relief, we should begin to formulate our aspirations for the coming year. What do we want and what can we achieve in 2013?

For those of us on the path of spiritual evolution, our cherished goal is for the freedom of higher consciousness. How does such a lofty goal translate to practical and achievable objectives?

Higher consciousness must perforce lead to changes in behavior, habit patterns and emotional maturity. Conversely, as one uses one's will to make changes to behavior patterns, one's consciousness changes. This is because we are overcoming our karmic predispositions.

The following is a list of achievable improvements in our external behavior which will promote a shift in mental and emotional patterns and lead to higher consciousness:

• 	maintaining a balance between spiritual and material life is necessary in dealing with the stress of modern living. A congenial means of acquiring the necessities of life for oneself and one's family complements our efforts in spiritual progress. It is best to avoid the temptation of avoiding one's duties in pursuit of personal liberation.

• 	maintaining a balance between our spiritual progress and our physical, emotional and mental well-being. The cultivation of self-healing techniques complements the techniques of Self-Realization. It is more difficulty to pursue spiritual evolution with a damaged vehicle.

• 	Develop a compassionate attitude towards all life, respecting the cycles of nature and refrain from violating the bounties of mother earth.

• 	Develop a loving attitude to all humanity - man and women, irrespective of color or caste, rich or poor, irrespective of religious or cultural affiliations.

• 	Resolve all conflicts whether with friends, relatives, co-workers or complete strangers from a non-violent base.

• 	Respect one's own body and mind by being discriminative in the influences that we allow to affect them. For the body, this requires an attention to our diet - less quantity and more on quality

- fresh and nutritious food in proper balance. For the mind, this requires paying attention to what movies and television shows we watch and what music we listen to.

The power of 2013 lies in the cultivation of Balance in all aspects. We will make more progress if we attune ourselves to this shift in energy. Happy New Year!

# Reflections For A Birthday

Every year, most of us experience a day of remembrance called the birthday. Yet, as we celebrate surviving another year of life, we wonder if there is any deeper significance beyond the cake, laughter and champagne. It is wonderful to be surrounded by those who care about you. When you are young, birthdays are exciting and something to look forward to. When one becomes old, they not only become tedious but in the West especially, something to be dreaded - a reminder of old age, wrinkles and infirmity. Can we salvage something spiritual from our birthday?

Just as the fear of death can be a great motivator on the spiritual path, gratitude for a human birth can inspire us to pursue an end to the cycle of birth and death. Every birthday reminds us that we are caught in a cycle of birth and death. We cannot remember where and what we were before our current birth. We do not know the purpose of our birth  - why are we born in a particular time and place? We do not know when this life will end. What we do know is that the Masters have said that a human birth is a precious opportunity to further our spiritual growth.

Let us examine what we are doing with our lives up to this moment. It is true that some of us are merely existing because we have no choice and are stuck here, reacting to external events as best we can in a sort of survival mode. However, most of us have certain material objectives depending on our age and circumstances. The young look for higher education, a good career, and a loving spouse to grow a family. The poor want to be rich. The rich want to be richer. The richest wish to fill the void in their souls through charities. The old look to a comfortable retirement. What are you living your life for? What do you do when you have achieved your material goals?

Let us remember the lesson from the conqueror Alexander of Macedonia who held the known world in his grasp. The young emperor on his death bed was instructed by his spiritual Master to be laid in state mourning with his open hands showing outside his royal coffin - to signify that we all come into this world with nothing and we leave with nothing. Pragmatically, we need to take care of our material needs but should leave space for the importance of our spiritual needs.

What are your spiritual objectives in this life? Some would like to live ethically, cultivating the higher virtues and human values. Some would like to help others and make a difference in lifting their society to greater well-being. Yet others perceive a fundamental shift of human consciousness is necessary to lift us from our selfish existence marked by fundamental suffering to an altruistic and wholistic worldview filled with living joy. Ultimately, we all want to know our purpose in this life but are afraid to find out because then we would have to do something about it!!

On this special day, once a year, we should strive to remember that life is not meaningless. Let us remember that we have choices. Let us remember that we are in a cycle of birth and death. Let us remember the teachings of the Masters. Let us remember the injunctions and practices of one's own Master. Let us remember the lessons of our spiritual experiences. Let us remember our spiritual goals. Let us remember to seek the blessings and grace of the Divine. Let us remember to offer our gratitude to the Divine. Let us surrender to the Divine will that guides us to our True Self. Let it be so!

# Finding Time for Practice

One of the greatest difficulties faced by the aspiring spiritual student is the lack of time that we all face in this busy age, especially in the more developed societies. It is one of the ironies that the average adult in the United States most probably has less free time then previous generations due to the stressful work environment and distracting media culture.

Of course, all sincere seekers have heard that maintaining a regular daily practice is the key to success in any of the many spiritual systems and this often leads to doubt in the sporadic efforts they can find in their busy schedule. However, where there is a will, there is a way.

All effective systems of Self-realization incorporate certain meditations that can be performed in any environment that you can close your eyes – in planes, trains, buses, waiting in line at the bank or doctor's office, during coffee break etc. What is needed is flexibility and determination.

Flexibility is needed to adapt to changing or adverse conditions while maintaining the essence of a practice. Determination is the will to look for and take advantage of any situation that may present itself for a practice session. Flexibility is the ability to modify or break up longer practices into short chunks to fit changing life conditions or emergency situations. Determination is the constant intent to expand one's consciousness.

It is important to grasp that spiritual practice is not an 'all or nothing' scenario. If you are supposed to give 45 minutes to a session but only have 25 minutes, don't just skip the session, make the most of the 25 minutes. Every little bit helps in spiritual evolution!

There is always some time before a meal that can be taken advantage of, especially, before breakfast or dinner. This helps to maintain a regular routine. Alternatively, take a shorter lunch break by practicing before eating a light lunch. Everyone has a different routines and constraints and must customize their practice accordingly.

Spiritual practice is a marathon, a long-term commitment and should be treated as such with forethought and planning. Make a plan for creating and maintaining this 'good habit.' The plan should consist of a series of possible practice sessions. Start with the ideal session – let us say, it is for one hour in the morning and one hour in the evening. Now make a session set that is only half an hour long in the morning and half an hour long in the evening. How about a fifteen minute long session? What can you do if you only have five minutes to sit on the park bench or a bus stop? What can you do if you have a one hour drive? Plan for these different scenarios and implement the one that fits the situation. You will always have some meditation or practice that you can make use of and so maintain the consciousness towards your spiritual goal.

One cannot make more time than one has, but we can take the skillful means to make the most of the time that presents itself for practice.

# Action With Awareness – Positive Conduct

*Rudra Shivananda*

Once an aspirant has set his or her foot on the spiritual path, a bewildering array of possibilities present themselves – the variety of spiritual groups, marketplace of systems, choice of teachers, myriad techniques and conflicting instructions. Choices to be made, doubts that constantly arise, and obstacles that present themselves are just more barriers to be overcome - as the seeker matures on the path, things don't necessary get easier or clearer!

What is going on? It is the illusionary trap that techniques and teachers are the most important factors on the path. Yes, they are very important and one should make careful choices and keep one's commitment, especially if one has the good karma to meet a Master. However, one's commitment to the Truth is the ultimate Light that can lead from ignorance to Self-Realization and losing sight of this Truth is the cause of the doubts and failure on the path.

Once a person realizes the value of a human birth with its potential for rapid spiritual evolution and consequently makes a dedication to higher consciousness, he or she needs to make an ultimate commitment to act in that higher consciousness.

How is it possible to act with higher consciousness when we have not achieved the higher states yet? That is where the teachings of the great sages come in. The great Masters have given us the spiritual values to live by – these values derive from their highest consciousness states and are based on the true reality. These values are not empty platitudes nor are they simple games for beginners - they are actually the most important part of our spiritual path, of any spiritual path. We must keep reminding ourselves that the goal of our evolutionary practice is to achieve our ultimate states of consciousness and the attendant wisdom that enables us to act in accordance with Universal Will. When we act with this awareness, we achieve peace and happiness.

*[200]*

All the confusion that comes about for sincere seekers arise because they have forgotten or neglected the ultimate truth that their present conduct in life mold their future consciousness. If we conduct ourselves negatively, we are sabotaging our spiritual practice. We must never lose sight of the importance of cultivating positive conduct in relationships, in our career, and in all aspects of our lives.

It is not finding the correct breathing technique, the true teacher or the most powerful mantra that will bring about the transformation of a human being to a Divine Being. Certainly, there is no doubt that finding a Master and being blessed with a spiritual practice are critical to the transformation process, but without the effort towards positive conduct, the process can delayed for life-times. Some Masters in the scriptures have even highlighted action with awareness as the key to unlocking our highest potential. The skillful seeker should keep this in mind and act accordingly – don't let yourself lose sight of the Truth because of ever-changing circumstances.

# Will versus Ego

There is frequently confusion among spiritual students about the role of the ego. Although there is an understanding that it is detrimental for spiritual growth, many believe that a strong ego is necessary to live successfully in this material world. They are therefore torn between the weakening of the ego from their spiritual practice and the fear that without the ego, they will be unable to support a family or even themselves. Such an internal conflict is due to the confusion between will and ego.

A strong will and the determination towards an objective is necessary for success in any endeavor. A strong ego can actually undermine the success and lead to disaster and failure. We can understand this be differentiating between the ego [*ahamkara* or I-maker] from the will power [*iccha Shakti*].

Ego drives a person to become defensive, to protect the self-image and leads to stubbornness and unwillingness to compromise or listen to constructive advice and feedback. Such a closed attitude eventually causes a breakdown and failure due to a divergence between the ego-centric worldview and the consensus reality – the "ego-reality gap". We can see this time and time again when a leader's initial success is transformed into later failure.

Will on the other hand is driven by vision and the power of higher consciousness. It leads to enthusiasm and determination to succeed in the manifestation of the vision. However, there is an open-ness and willingness to work with others, changing cherished plans for the sake of the goal. The ego would rather sabotage a project rather than share the credit or admit any limitations, whereas a strong leader will encourage everyone for the sake of the shared objective.

A strong leader is motivating, tolerant and helpful. An egotistical leader is fearful of others, putting them down at every opportunity, vengeful for minor hurts and rules by fear.

The problems of the world, whether between countries , between co-workers or between family members are all caused by the collision of egos and can be overcome by the strength and will that is driven by higher consciousness instead.
For the spiritual students, their spiritual practice will purify their minds and weaken the ego. This allows higher consciousness to awaken and strengthen their will power. This will power is what should be developed in order to persevere in their practice as well as succeed in the more material concerns of a householder life.

Vigilance and awareness is necessary to differentiate between our ego-centric thoughts, words and speech and those powered by will-power. We should observe for any interference from the ego and overcome them by centering ourselves in higher consciousness.

# Life Goal - Immortality or Divinity?

There are diverse reasons for seekers to pursue a spiritual path – some are striving for liberation from pain and suffering, others are seeking knowledge of their their true nature and reason for being, and yet others want freedom from death and to achieve immortality. Of course, it may be reasoned that all these goals can converge and are not conflicting with each other. However, the confusion in the minds of seekers over their final objective can impede their progress on the path and also lead to pursuit of illusionary ways and means.

It is taught by the sages that our essential nature is divine and that the pursuit of True Self will lead to the experience of our divinity in the sense of freedom from limitations that plague the human condition, including that of death. It is a given that immortality is an attribute of divinity. Other attributes include freedom from desires and negativities and universal knowledge and wisdom. We are not talking about the attaining to the state of angelic beings who are are designated as devas or light beings in the timeless teachings of the ancients. Our True Self is beyond that of these devas who themselves are on the path of realizing themselves.

Although the attainment of our divinity bestows immortality, the path may seem long and arduous to many seekers. Even in the ancient times, there arose diverse paths that focus on the attainment of immortality and freedom from death.

The sages gave their teachings in the Upanshads that focused on the atman or spirit – our True Self. In the Katha Upanishad, the hero Nachiketas refused the gift of physical immortality in order to learn the secret of attainment of liberation into divinity. The theme of the sages is consistent – only the spirit or atman is truly immortal and beyond the karmic bonds of life and death, pain and suffering. Even the long-lived devas have a finite existence – some will last the life of a galaxy while a few till the dissolution of the universe. The theme of spiritual immortality is a central one taught by Lord Krishna in the Bhagavadgita. It is the spirit than is beyond death and cannot be harmed by the elements.

As humanity descended into deeper ignorance, there arose a greater longing to evade physical death and prolong a particular life-time. Stories of immortal beings were used as examples of the possibility to attain physical immortality and various means were prescribed, such as the use of magical herbs or chemical compounds made from mercury and sulfur to transform the decayable body. Stories of successful transformations formed the basis for generation upon generation of experimentation. However, such pursuits merely tended to side-track the spiritual student from the path of liberation.

The Naths and Siddhas – upholders of the many yogic paths for thousands of years have been responsible for preserving the teachings of the great masters. However, their writings are often couched in coded and abstruse words to prevent those with impure motives to misuse them. Some of these writings on alchemy are often cited as supporting the path of physical immortality. Indeed, many of the Naths and Siddhas were able to transform their bodies into adamantine or non-decaying nature and lived for many generations in order to do some great work for humanity. However, we need to keep in mind that they all achieved liberation in their life-time before they transformed their bodies – they attained their divinity first.

Indeed, the founder of the Naths, Mahavatar Gorakshanth, has pointed out in his Amanaska Yoga, that in order to attain an immortal body, one must transcend the limitations such as carnality, hunger, thirst, sleep, disease, old age etc. He has also said that the attainment of a vajra-deha or immortal body is only possible when one has attained akhand samadhi or an unbroken and sustained realization of the True Self.

Therefore, one should only aim for divinity – immortality follows divinity and not necessarily the other way around. Indeed, striving for immortality before attaining Divine Realization is the ultimate trap for the advanced practitioner and will impede spiritual evolution.

# Listen To Your Inner Guide

### To Make A Difficult Choice

How often are we faced with a situation where we are called upon to decide between the lesser of two choices that both have negative consequences? We often wish that we can just stop and not to choose and do nothing at all. Sometimes the consequences are minor while other times, even inaction can have huge impact.

Recently, there has been a lot of public handwringing about choosing between the two candidates for the upcoming presidential election. Both candidates are considered flawed by supporters as well as opponents with both having high un-favorability ratings.

Some potential voters are somewhat stressed or depressed because they have difficulty rationalizing a decision while others are equally fervent in knowing what they think they want, even though their minds are being tugged in conflicting directions.

The situation of a conflicted mind reminds me of the classic example that is the basis for the spiritual text called Bhagavad Gita. This text is the insight into the meaning of life with the means to acquiring wisdom and skill in action. The first chapter is called the 'Despondency of Arjuna' and sets up the scenario for the exposition by the embodiment of divinity, Lord Krishna.

Arjuna represents us – his mind is confused with discordant thoughts and he requires guidance. He lacks the power of discrimination that would enable him to make the right choices in life.

The Bhagavad Gita takes place at the beginning of a battle between close relatives. The consequence of the upcoming battle has just dawned on Arjuna. He has just realized that he has to choose between two conflicting duties. The first is his duty as a prince to uphold righteousness and battle evil. However, he has an equally strong duty to defend and protect family members. What happens when one is faced with the situation that it is one's family members who are unrighteous and performing evil actions?

Arjuna's mind is stalled by thoughts of fighting his elders, teachers and cousins or letting them kill his brothers and friends. He throws down his arms in despair and would rather not do anything. Unfortunately, he realizes that his inaction is a choice and might mean the demise of his brothers. He therefore connects with his inner guide who has taken form as a charioteer, Lord Krishna and asks for his help.

Lord Krishna uses the rest of the Gita to explain the means by which a person can attain to the wisdom of higher consciousness and utilize discriminative intellect to live a life in tune with the will of the Divine. The wisdom of the Gita is timeless and is a source of guidance for us even now. It can help us to:

- Act freely and unconditionally

- Have confidence in the power and guidance of the goodness within the universe

- Choose between unclear alternatives to resolve dilemmas that we face

To paraphrase the Gita, the wise person unites his or her actions with insight (buddhi) and so is not bound by the results or karmic consequences. Yoga is skill in action. Persons who are wise and have insight into their own natures have no need to be told what to do. Whenever you're conflicted and your mind is torn between choices, remember the lessons of the Gita and seek practice and knowledge to achieve yoga.

# Conclusion - Beginning

It is my sincere hope that the contents of this book have been helpful to you, the reader. If you enjoyed it, all the better!

The journey does not end until time itself is transcended, therefore there is no conclusion and no beginning. It is a process to Being which just Is, when That Is Now and only Now. Sounds strange, but there It Is.

My advice is to break up routine and habit, expecially those that impede your spiritual progress and open your heart and soul to new dimensions of soul experience. Words are insufficient but that's what we have to work with.

Don't take refuge in ideas and philosophies, however lofty - remember that it is how we treat our fellow human beings in good times and in bad times that is a measure of our spiritual progress. Indeed, good thoughts should be followed by good words and deeds.

Remember to forgive yourself as your forgive others.

The following page is blank - every moment is a new beginning.

Good Journey!

# Books by Rudra Shivananda

Chakra selfHealing by the Power of Om

Yoga of Purification and Transformation

Surya Yoga - Healing by Solar Power

Breathe Like Your Life Depends On It

In Light of Kriya Yoga

Healing Postures of the 18 Siddhas

Insight and Guidance for Spiritual Seekers

Practical Mantra Yoga

Breathe Better Live Longer

Nada: The Yoga of Inner Sound

Living A Spiritual Life In A Material World

website: www.rudrashivananda.com
blog: www.sanatanamitra.com
www.youtube.com/user/KriyaNathYogi

# About the Author

Rudra Shivananda, a disciple of the Himalayan GrandMaster Yogiraj Siddhanath, is dedicated to the service of humanity through the furthering of human awareness and spiritual evolution. He teaches that the only lasting way to bring happiness into one's life is by a consistent practice of awareness and transformation. He has developed healing programs utilizing the energy centers [Chakras] and Prana Energy techniques through breath.

Rudra Shivananda is committed to spreading the message of the immortal Being called Babaji. He teaches the message of World and Individual Peace through the practice of Kriya Yoga. As a student and teacher of yoga for more than 40 years, he is trained as an Acharya or Spiritual Preceptor in the Indian Nath Tradition, closely associated with the Siddha tradition. He lives in the San Francisco Bay area, and has given initiations and workshops in USA, Ireland, England, Japan, Spain, Brazil, Russia, Singapore, Malaysia, Hong Kong, India, Australia, Canada and Estonia.